FIFTY WAYS TO AVOID MALPRACTICE

A Guidebook for Mental Health Professionals

ROBERT HENLEY WOODY, PhD, ScD, JD

Professional Resource Exchange, Inc.
Sarasota, Florida

Printed in the United States of America

Paperbound Edition ISBN: 0-943158-54-0
Library of Congress Catalog Number: 88-42814

The copy editor for this book was Janet Sailian, the pro-
duction supervisor was Debbie Fink, the graphics coordi-
nator was Judy Warinner, the cover designer was Bill Tab-
ler, and the printer was Edwards Brothers, Inc.

Dedication

To my mother and father,
Wilma and Robert Woody;

To my wife,
Jane Divita Woody;

To our children,
Jennifer, Robert III, and Matthew Woody.

A Cautionary Note

This book is intended to provide accurate and authoritative information about its subject. It is sold with the understanding that the publisher and the author are not engaged in rendering legal, accounting, or other professional service. If legal advice or other expert assistance is required, the services of a competent professional, with knowledge of all laws pertaining to the reader, should be sought.

The Author

Robert Henley Woody is a practicing attorney and psychologist, with offices in Omaha, NE, Fort Myers, FL, and Grand Rapids, MI ("Of Counsel" with the law firm of Bergstrom, Quinn, & Oole, P.A.). His law practice emphasizes protecting health care professionals from ethical, regulatory, and legal complaints. He also conducts seminars on risk management and avoiding malpractice in health care services for universities, professional organizations, hospitals, and clinics.

Dr. Woody is a Professor of Psychology and Social Work and Director of School Psychology Training at the University of Nebraska at Omaha, and Adjunct Professor of Psychiatry at Michigan State University. Previously, he was Dean for Graduate Studies and Research at the University of Nebraska at Omaha, an Assistant Professor at the State University of New York at Buffalo, an Associate Professor at the University of Maryland, Dean of Student Development at Grand Valley State College, and Professor at the Ohio University. He was a Visiting Professor at the University of Reading (England) and the Ohio State University.

Dr. Woody received his Doctor of Philosophy degree in counseling psychology from Michigan State University (1964), his Doctor of Science degree in health services administration and research from the University of Pittsburgh (1975), and his Juris Doctor degree from the Creighton University School of Law (1981). During 1966-1967, he was a Post-Doctoral Fellow in Clinical Psychology at the University of London's Institute of Psychiatry (Maudsley Hospital), and in 1969 he received the Two-Year Post-Doctoral Certificate in Group Psychotherapy from the Washington School of Psychiatry.

Dr. Woody is admitted by the Nebraska, Michigan, and Florida state bars for the practice of law, and is a licensed psychologist in the same states. He holds a Diplomate in Clinical Psychology with the American Board of Professional Psychology, a Diplomate in Forensic Psychology with the American Board of Forensic Psychology, and a Diplomate in (Experimental) Psychological Hypnosis with the American Board of Psychological Hypnosis. He is a Fellow of the American Psychological Association, the American Association for Marriage and Family Therapy, the Society for Personality Assessment, the National Academy of Neuropsychologists, and the American Society of Clinical Hypnosis.

Dr. Woody has authored or edited 20 books and approximately 300 articles for professional journals. His books include *Protecting Your Mental Health Practice* (1988), *Becoming a Clinical Psychologist* (with Malcolm Robertson, 1988), *Health Promotion in Family Therapy* (with James R. Springer, 1985), *The Law and the Practice of Human Services* (1984), *Sexual Issues in Family Therapy* (with Jane Divita Woody, 1983), and *The Encyclopedia of Clinical Assessment* (1980).

Table of Contents

Preface

Our society demands qualitative accountability from all practitioners vested with the cloak of professionalism. Public policy once entrusted quality control to self-regulation by professional organizations, such as through requiring members to adhere to ethical standards. In the 1960s, mental health services proliferated, and the mental health disciplines started seeking state licensure. This led to governmental regulations (such as through licensing boards). By the mid-1970s, our society became alarmed at the increasing number of incidents involving abuse of or injury to clients/patients caused by health practitioners, and the malpractice era dawned. Today, all health care providers (including mental health practitioners) face stringent policing by professional ethics committees, state departments of professional regulation (including licensing boards), and courts of law.

After two decades as a clinical, counseling, and school psychologist, I earned a Juris Doctor degree and became an attorney. Prior to my legal training, I was largely unaware of the legal implications of day-to-day mental health practice. As I shared my legal knowledge with my mental health colleagues, I found that many, perhaps most, mental health practitioners lack adequate understanding of the law, notwithstanding that the press from ethical, regulatory, and legal sanctions continues to increase.

The outcome has been my commitment to teach mental health professionals to practice proactively in a manner that will minimize the possibility of complaints. My work has centered on providing legal representation to (as well as consultation to attorneys representing) health care providers. I have conducted seminars on risk management and avoiding malpractice in mental health services for a wide variety of professional groups. I have been fortunate to be involved with many cases that reveal the pathways to problems. From these experiences, I have created a map for avoiding the quagmire of malpractice. This book traces the 50-step route to malpractice avoidance.

The first three chapters emphasize public policy and legal principles. Chapter 1, "The Escalation of Professional Liability," defines malpractice and describes the magnitude of the problem, the causes of action (the reasons for which you can be sued), and the self-defeating conflicts engaged in by health care and legal professionals. Malpractice insurance is explained, and the nature (both overt and covert) of the insurance industry is revealed. Chapter 2, "The Mental Health Professional in Society," explores society's expectation of professionals, as manifested in health care policy and professional regulation, and emphasizes conceptualizing contemporary mental health services as a business. A brief introduction to the legal system is also provided. Chapter 3, "Negligence and Standard of Care," explains public policy and negligence theory, the requisite elements for establishing negligence, remedies for a negligence complaint, defenses available to the defendant-practitioner, legal principles for determining the standard of care for clinical practice, and vicarious liability.

The final five chapters present 50 specific guidelines for avoiding malpractice in the provision of mental health services. Chapter 4, "The Professional-Self Concept," focuses on being what you are prepared to be professionally, professional development, personal monitoring, and relevant business practices. Chapter 5, "The Company That You Keep," highlights vicarious liability; that is, how you can be sued for a wrongful act by a colleague or associate. Chapter 6, "Framing a Clinical Practice," specifies means for structuring and maintaining a practice that minimizes malpractice liability. Chapter 7, "Client Management," tells how to gain legal protection by informed consent, preventive strategies, and client compliance. Chapter 8, "Healthy Defensiveness," points out that this litigious era justifies precautionary measures by every mental health practitioner.

The material in the book comes from an extensive analysis of statutory and case law, research and writings, psycholegal experiences with health care professionals (for whom I have served as attorney or legal consultant in their trying times), and interactions with participants in my seminars. The result is a wealth of material that has not heretofore been brought together. Knowing that the mental health practitioner holds time to be precious and places priority on practical information, I have sought to present the relevant legal principles and describe the implications as briefly as possible without sacrificing scholarship, and to pinpoint the practical strategies available for immediate implementation by the practitioner.

The book is structured to present public policy and legal theory (in the first three chapters), and then to reiterate the important issues in the context of guidelines for practices (in the next five chapters). The guidelines thus contain information on policy and theory similar to what was presented earlier in the book; the repetition clarifies application to practice and reinforces acquisition of the strategies.

This book is intended primarily for the mental health practitioner, be he or she in clinical, counseling, or school psychology; social work; mental health counseling; marriage and family therapy; sex therapy; pastoral counseling; psychiatry; nursing; or whatever. The book does not have to be read in full, though this may be the best way to acquire both the academic rationale and the practical techniques; it is designed to allow the reader to extract relevant material as a guideline for a particular problem.

The book is also suited for university and professional training in the various mental health disciplines. Given the critical nature of the legal-ethical interface with mental health practice, every student/trainee should be familiar with ethical, regulatory, and legal complaints and ways that they can be avoided. Such knowledge benefits the practitioner, the client, and our society. The book can serve as a text for any advanced practice course, particularly one dealing with ethical and legal issues.

I express my appreciation to my clients and colleagues, and to seminar participants, who have helped me formulate my ideas and offered me the benefit of their ethical and legal experiences. I have received special support from Drs. Jane Divita Woody, James R. Springer,

Paul G. Schauble, Robert B. Silver, James C. Hansen, and David C. Regester. Through the ongoing publication of my "Psycholegal Notebook" in *The Florida Psychologist*, each member of the Florida Psychological Association, and particularly Robert Hall (Executive Director), has furthered the development of the ideas contained in this book. I hope that this book will allow other mental health professionals to learn how to provide legally safe and ethically acceptable services.

R.H.W.

Omaha, NE,
Fort Myers, FL,
and Grand Rapids, MI
April, 1988

FIFTY WAYS TO AVOID MALPRACTICE

A Guidebook for Mental Health Professionals

Chapter 1:
The Escalation of
Professional Liability

Mental health services comprise an essential sector of
the national health care system. While the government-
sponsored community mental health programs of the 1960s
have dwindled, there continues to be rapid growth of free-
enterprise mental health services. Although financially
unfeasible and poorly regulated a decade or so ago, today
private practice is a viable career option for professionals
of every mental health discipline. More recently, health
maintenance organizations (HMOs) and related ventures
are replacing the solo or group practice with a complex
corporate structure. Many mental health services already
constitute "big business," and they have merged with the
"health industry."

One of the hallmark indicators of the success of mental health services is the number of practitioners accepted
into health care settings that were once the exclusive
territory of physicians. But employment in the health
care field has been the proverbial double-edged sword:
On one side, there are the benefits of practicing in a
comprehensive medical/health care program; on the other
side, this association with medicine has led to an
increased willingness on the part of clients or patients to
sue the mental health practitioner (Knapp & VandeCreek,
1981).

Complaints against mental health practitioners can be
directed to: (a) the practitioner for attempted self-
resolution; (b) an ethics committee (at the local, regional,
state, or national level) for a directive from the practition-

er's disciplinary organization; (c) a state regulatory agency (including the licensing board) for disciplinary action; or (d) a court of law for a judgment and (presumably) an award of damages in a civil action or a conviction and sentence in a criminal action. It is possible, of course, for a complaint to be processed by more than one of these sources.

The broad area of avoiding a complaint is known as *risk management*. Among other things, the mental health practitioner engaged in risk management considers being adequately insured; making wise investments; defining an appropriate scope of practice and standard of care; defining policies with ethical, regulatory, and legal safeguards; selecting a useful business form or entity; using carefully planned marketing and advertising methods; managing human resources and accounts wisely; maintaining effective operations; and avoiding malpractice. The purpose of risk-management techniques is to avoid complaints to professional ethics committees, governmental regulatory agencies, and courts of laws.

Risk management has been the topic of another recent book of mine titled *Protecting Your Mental Health Practice* (1988). That book emphasizes protective and proactive business strategies. This book is more focused, and deals specifically with avoiding malpractice in clinical mental health services.

DEFINING MALPRACTICE

The price of "professionalism" levied by public policy is *fulfillment of a duty to provide adequate quality care*, as based on what is deemed to be acceptable to a reasonable and prudent mental health professional. Chapter 3 dissects this fundamental premise, and recasts it into a *standard of care*. When adequate quality care is not provided, public policy endorses accountability, such as by authorizing a client to file a malpractice suit.

Malpractice is the failure to fulfill the requisite standard of care. Malpractice can occur by *omission* (what should have been done, but was not done) or *commission* (doing something that should not have been done). In either case, the act is not subject to a malpractice legal action unless it satisfies the elements for negligence, namely that there was a duty which was breached and which caused injury to a person to whom the duty was owed, and damages can be used to remedy the tortious infringement on the injured person's rights. Chapter 3 provides details on negligence theory, and how it applies to malpractice in mental health services.

THE MAGNITUDE OF THE PROBLEM

With the problem identified, our analysis can move forward by considering how extensive the problem is for today's mental health professional.

From the onset, it must be acknowledged that the true magnitude of the problem is not known—there is no all-encompassing statistic. Part of this void is due to the fact that many disputes that could lead to malpractice action are resolved between the parties, and no public record is available for statistical purposes. For example, a client may want to avoid paying for treatment and will claim that the therapist did not provide adequate treatment. Sensing that a dispute is not worth the hassle, the therapist will simply tell the client that the bill will be eliminated; this may keep the client from considering the therapist's faults, which could lead to a malpractice claim.

Another frequent scenario involves an attorney formulating a legal action, approaching the professional (or his or her employer or insurance carrier), and offering to settle the matter without filing with the court. Or going a step further, a case that has been filed will, upon settlement, be dismissed with the stipulation that the terms of the settlement be kept confidential. Again, no public records are available.

Based on a retrospective study of 25 years of professional liability coverage for psychologists, Wright (1981) concluded that the majority (more than 75%) of claims against psychologists fell in the nuisance category and were settled for less than $5,000 including legal costs. Presumably the amount is higher today.

For legitimate medical malpractice cases, Jacobs (1978, 1986) indicates that—given a good attorney, a record review, and an expert to testify about the standard of care and damages—about 80% of the cases will be settled; of the remainder that go to trial, about one-third will be settled during the trial.

Whether these same percentages would apply to the various mental health disciplines remains for conjecture, but the principle probably holds up: Most complaints can and will be settled, even though the emotional and financial expenses will still be present.

From American Psychological Association (APA) records, Fisher (1985) reported that from 1955 to 1965 (the first 10 years that malpractice insurance coverage was offered to the APA membership) there were no claims. Between 1976 and 1981, there was an average of 44 claims per year. From 1982 to 1984, there was an average of 153 claims per year. She cites the insurance carrier (the American Professional Agency) as saying that "the number of claims against psychologists have risen faster in the past three years than for any other mental health profession" (p. 6).

Complaints are also increasing against marriage and family therapists (cf., the "Legal Consultation Plan Newsletter" of the American Association for Marriage and Family Therapy), counselors, school personnel, and social workers (Besharov, 1985; Fischer & Sorenson, 1985). At this time, it appears that any mental health professional can be a target for malpractice complaints.

Why is there an increase in complaints? Two reasons deserve comment at this point, and others will be mentioned later.

First, mental health services involve a good deal of subjectivity. Drawing from an inexact science, mental health professionals differ greatly in their uses of diagnostic and treatment techniques. Simply put, there is no uniform, objectively selected, controlled application of mental health practice procedures or conditions. The variability leads to an often ill-defined and poorly formulated standard of care. Public policy requires more of mental health professionals.

Second, mental health professionals are trained in varying disciplines, each of which has its own disciplinary identity, objectives, and training standards:

> To further complicate matters, the mental health profession is not homogeneous. Its diverse practitioners have completed varying educational programs and are licensed and organized into disparate groups. Commonly recognized practitioners include psychiatrists, psychologists, psychotherapists, psychoanalysts, school psychologists, clinical social workers, licensed social workers, psychiatric social workers, mental health counselors, marriage therapists, marriage counselors, marriage consultants, family therapists, family counselors, family consultants, sex therapists, sex counselors, grief

counselors, and behavior modification specialists. (Leesfield, 1987, p. 57)

The list of mental health identities could probably go on and on.

Notwithstanding this inconsistency of training, role definition, or purposes, whenever a legal action is taken against a member of any one of these mental health disciplines, there is an apparent spill over to the other mental health identities. For example, the legal principle of "duty to warn" was accentuated by a case involving a psychologist in a university counseling center, but it has since been extended to essentially every mental health professional in whatever employment context.

Whether there is or is not a "crisis" and why mental health professionals are meeting up with litigious clients is addressed later in this chapter. An analysis of the causes of action in the next section reveals the kinds of errors or *faux pas* that can justify a client's complaints about a mental health professional.

The escalation of liability indicates the contemporary importance placed on mental health services. In the eyes of the public, mental health professionals possess a peerless and unprecedented degree of responsibility and status. As mental health services have become part of the fabric of our society, professionals have become subject to greater liability.

As but one example of their new-found "success," mental health professionals are now working in medical settings. As cited earlier, Knapp and VandeCreek (1981) believe that the behavioral-medicine framework, in which many mental health professionals currently operate, creates greater malpractice risk than was present in more traditional mental health care. In the past, mental health clients may have been reluctant to sue because of the stigma attached to receiving mental health services. Today, clients do not hesitate to "go public" with a history of having received treatment. In addition, physically ill patients (being treated in a medical setting) may not have experienced the kind of therapeutic alliance or relationship that would deter them from suing the mental health professional.

A more obvious example of "success" is in the realm of finances. When a would-be claimant approaches an attorney, the legal analysis appropriately includes the probability of recovering damages. If the case is solid *but*

5

the defendant has few assets, the attorney is likely to be less willing to file a lawsuit than if the defendant is known (or apt) to have malpractice insurance or other assets that can be obtained by a judgment for the plaintiff. For example, the expenses associated with a lawsuit (such as hiring experts to testify about the alleged breach of the standard of mental health care) would make it illogical to proceed against a professional with no malpractice insurance coverage or few assets. On the other hand, if the case is solid *and* the defendant has substantial assets, the proverbial "deep pocket" that is needed to gain compensation for the plaintiff is present.

A judgment for the plaintiff can tap the assets of the mental health professional and his or her associates, employer (vicarious liability will be discussed later), or insurance carrier. The mental health professions, compared to other careers, offer a good income, a fact that makes these professionals prime targets for legal actions. The financial issue is undoubtedly an important part of the escalation of liability. If mental health professionals were disenfranchised financially, it is quite likely that public policy would lessen their liability.

CAUSES OF ACTION

In legal parlance, a *cause of action* in the context of a legal complaint against a mental health professional refers to a matter that can be contested or litigated under a publicly accepted legal theory and governing framework. In the case of a legal complaint (such as a malpractice suit), the allegation is that the professional has violated statutory or common law.

A legal cause of action must be consonant with the laws of the particular state, commonly even when the case is brought in the federal courts (with some exceptions). If the cause of action is not adequately supported by law, the case may be dismissed.

If the attorney who files a case knew or should have known that it is an improper cause of action, many jurisdictions allow the defendant to file an *abuse of process* action against the plaintiff's attorney or a *malicious prosecution* action against the plaintiff. Taking solace from the notion of a countersuit is not advisable, however, since this sort of suit is generally very difficult to win. For example, Florida law recognizes actions for malicious prosecution, but such actions are "not favored by the courts." There are demanding criteria that must be fulfilled to sustain a countersuit and obtain a judgment based on, say, malicious prosecution or abuse of process.

Many different causes of actions have been asserted against mental health professionals. A summary review of these follows.

An important review of malpractice cases against psychotherapists (of all mental health disciplines) has been completed by Hogan (1979). Concerning causes of action, he states:

> Despite the myriad actions available, the simple negligence or malpractice suit is by far the most preferred by plaintiffs, occurring in more than half of all cases, and more than five times as frequently as the next most common legal action, which is deprivation of one's constitutional rights (11.3 percent). After these two, an assortment of actions exists, ranging from false imprisonment (8.0 percent) to administrative law (less than 1 percent). Occasionally suits are brought for false arrest, trespass, malicious infliction of emotional distress, abuse of process, and misrepresentation. (p. 18)

Hogan identified more than 25 types of action, and cited, in addition to those listed above, "involuntary servitude, false arrest, trespass, malicious infliction of emotional distress, abuse of process, loss of liberty, misrepresentation, libel, assault and battery, malicious prosecution, and false imprisonment" (p. 7) as being reasons for legal actions against psychotherapists. Similarly, Trent (1978) reviewed claims filed against psychiatrists, identifying improper hospital commitments, death, pressing for fee collection, subpoenas to testify, sexual relations with patients, adverse drug reactions, unauthorized release of confidential information causing damage to the patient, suicide, improper administrative handling, electroconvulsive therapy, improper treatment, and injury to a nonpatient during therapy.

With all respect to Hogan and Trent, it should be noted that these surveys encompassed cases that were decades old. Each aforementioned cause of action is, however, still relevant, and could potentially be a cause of action today.

In a more recent survey of malpractice claims against social workers (derived from claims made under a policy issued by the American Home Assurance Company to members of the National Association of Social Workers), Besharov (1985) identified, by rank order of number of cases: (a) sexual impropriety; (b) incorrect treatment; (c) improper child placement; (d) breach of confidentiality; (e) improper death of patient or others; (f) child placement removal (including custody disputes); (g) violation of civil rights; (h) bodily injury to client; (i) defamation (libel or slander); (j) failure to supervise client properly, causing injury to client or other; (k) suicide of patient; (l) failure to make or improper diagnosis; (m) countersuit (due to fee collection); (n) false imprisonment (improper hospitalization); (o) breach of contract; (p) assault and battery; (q) failure to warn of client's dangerousness; (r) abandonment of client; (s) failure to cure (poor results); (t) failure to refer; (u) accident on premises; (v) licensing or peer review; (w) undue influence; and miscellaneous other reasons.

This list of reasons for malpractice actions against social workers seems comprehensive. From a knowledge of malpractice actions against professionals from the other mental health disciplines, there is no reason to believe that these causes of action are unique to social workers—each one could be applied to psychiatrists, psychologists, mental health counselors, or other types of mental health professionals. Moreover, although seemingly comprehensive, each category could potentially be renamed, and an enterprising attorney is prepared to create a new cause of action from established statutory or case law.

The most cursory perusal of this list of malpractice claims reveals how far-reaching professional liability is under today's malpractice law. As will emerge, the reach is constantly extending further and further. For example, the failure to refer seems to be a more common reason for actions today than in the past, and it is being extended to failure to follow-up (as relevant to "abandonment").

Sexual contact with a patient is a major reason for litigation against mental health professionals, and so-called "sexual misconduct" malpractice suits are increasing (Pope & Bouhoutsos, 1986). Fisher (1985) reports that during "the past two years, the number of sexual malpractice suits against psychologists have multiplied by five, so that they represent 20 to 30 percent of all suits, and cost insurers twice as much as all other causes combined" (p. 7). While this type of malpractice involves primarily male mental health professionals, Turkington (1984) points out that female therapists are not immune to sexual involvement suits, although these most often involve a female (not a male) client's complaint about a female therapist.

The involvement of third-party payments, that is, having mental health services paid for by health insurance, introduces another source of potential litigation which could lead to further escalation of liability: the peer review process. It is now standard practice to have insurance claims from health care providers subjected to "peer review." This imposes a critical analysis that could reveal faulty case management, and thereby create a basis for a complaint. For example, the insurance company hires a mental health professional to evaluate and monitor claims for reimbursement for psychotherapy. In a similar vein, the development of employment assistance programs (EAPs) adds complexity to mental health services in the form of the patient's employer and possibly an insurance carrier being concerned about the quality of care being provided. Under this arrangement, the employer directly supports the costs of mental health services for employees by contracting with professionals to render the services. This leads to new sources monitoring accountability for quality, and they could assume the role of plaintiff.

The body of law relevant to third-party involvement is still growing, and exactly how it will take shape is unknown. There are, however, many possible pitfalls for the mental health professional. For example, if an employer or insurance company is paying for the treatment, there could be an expectation of receiving information from the professional about the employee-client and about the cost effectiveness of the therapy expenditure. The client's expectation and presumed right to confidentiality and privileged communication could be at stake. Even if well-intentioned, a mental health professional's faulty handling of confidential and privileged information could embroil him or her in legal controversy.

As an example of how a health insurance company can confront a mental health professional, Verrillo (1987) reports that the Alabama Blue Cross/Blue Shield has charged 11 mental health professionals with allegedly filing fraudulent insurance claims, and is seeking $1.1 million dollars in damages. A representative of the American Mental Health Counselors Association interpreted the action as revealing the insurance company's assumption that psychotherapy is "outside the lawful scope of the licensed professional counselor" (p. 1). Apparently, some Alabama mental health counselors filed reimbursement claims under the signature and supervision of a physician or clinical psychologist, and the insurance carrier now views "this standard and commonly accepted practice as illegal" (p. 8). Reportedly, Blue Cross companies in other states view this matter differently. The outcome of this case is yet to be determined, but it reveals an adversarial relationship between a health insurance carrier and mental health care providers stemming from different views on which mental health disciplines are qualified to provide reimbursable psychotherapy.

Another example of skepticism, if not conflict, between a health insurance carrier and a mental health professional occurred in a family therapy clinic. All clients filing insurance claims were seen by a family physician, and he signed the insurance claim forms. The insurance company detected that he was not a psychiatrist and demanded documentation of his training to supervise psychotherapy. Had the family physician failed to satisfy the health insurance company, one might speculate about whether or not he would have faced charges of fraud. Of course, had the insurance carrier denied reimbursement, the therapists would likely have incurred the rancor of clients burdened with a larger personal payment than had been expected.

The message about third-party payments is simple. When a source other than the client is involved in the mental health service, especially in providing the pay- ment, there exists a fertile plot for the sprouting of legal complaints.

INTERDISCIPLINARY CONFLICTS

It would seem that all professionals committed to human service (e.g., attorneys, physicians, mental health professionals, and other human service and health care professionals) would sense a camaraderie and band together in the face of the so-called malpractice crisis. Such is not the case.

The escalation of liability has led to great dissonance between the legal profession and all of the health care professions. As will be presented in later sections, there may be another source that is, for whatever reason, making matters worse between attorneys and health care professionals: the insurance industry.

For example, consider the case where an attorney received for his client a $3 million out-of-court settlement from a hospital for faulty neurosurgery and use of a CAT Scanner: "The right and left sides of the film were reversed, and normal brain tissue from a 16-year-old girl was removed," leaving permanent short-term memory loss (McCarthy, 1986, p. 2). As part of the settlement agreement, the attorney made a pledge to advertise the problem to alert other hospital staffs, hopefully to help them avoid such errors and legal consequences. Reportedly he mailed an advertisement (with payment) to the *New England Journal of Medicine*, but the advertisement was refused, and rejection slips from other medical publications followed.

In certain locales, computer-based searches can be conducted to identify the litigation history of a physician. Conversely, the same type of searches are available for a physician to trace the litigation history of a patient. Such practices bear witness to the atmosphere of declared warfare.

Professional health care organizations, such as the American Medical Association, make recommendations and lobby for legislation that will limit legal liability—even for professionals who are, in fact, negligent and who damage patients. In turn, legal organizations, such as the American Bar Association and the Association of Trial Lawyers of America, counter with recommendations and lobbying efforts to better define legal liability. Efforts by legal sources to define liability are often interpreted by health care professionals and the insurance industry as being intended to expand liability, as opposed to improving the legal rights of both health care providers and patients.

Defensiveness, suspicion, and all-out hostility are common between attorneys and health care providers. Yet an occasional bright spot emerges in this arena of warring professionals. Especially noteworthy, some local medical and legal associations are coming together to create a medical-legal code. For example, the legal and medical groups in one locale formed a committee, stating:

> The purpose of the Medical/Legal Liaison Committee is to promote better communications and understanding between physicians and attorneys; pro-

mote the welfare and well-being of the patient or client and establish guidelines that conform with the highest code of ethics consistent with both professions. The joint Committee also endeavors to conciliate any dispute between members . . . of the two professions. (Lee County Bar Association/Lee County Medical Society, 1986, p. 1)

This cooperative stance is certainly a long-overdue step in the right direction. The message is clear: It seems wise for mental health professionals to seek the same sort of liaison with the legal community.

MALPRACTICE INSURANCE

The notion of a "malpractice crisis" is based, for the most part, on the ever-rising cost of malpractice insurance. A related index is the number of lawsuits filed against a health care profession.

First, it must be acknowledged that some clients have terrible and tragic experiences in receiving health care. Sometimes these are accidental; sometimes they reflect the character or competency of the health care provider. To exemplify the problem from the perspective of the consumer-patient, Hallerstein (1984) reports on survey data that reveal: 36% of patients admitted to hospitals developed new illnesses as a result of the treatment they received; serious errors occurred with 9%; and unexpected death occurred with 2%.

Public policy has endorsed that clients (or their families and estates) should receive compensation for certain damages suffered due to health care providers. Because public policy makes the legal system readily accessible to citizen consumers or clients, health care professionals are generally willing to purchase insurance for protection.

The essence of purchasing malpractice insurance is captured in the title of Turkington's (1986a) article, "Response to Crisis: Pay Up or Go Naked." She reports that the cost of malpractice insurance is rising. For example, the malpractice policy offered by a New Hampshire psychological association for $750 in 1984 cost $4,000 by 1986. "Going Naked" refers to having no liability insurance. As for individual psychologists, she indicates that in 1976, the malpractice insurance policy available through the American Psychological Association cost $70 per year. In 1986, restrictions are placed on writing policies, and the annual premium for psychologists is reportedly around $500. Certain "insurance watchers" believe the cost will go substantially higher. "APA officials, although unhappy with the $450 premium, realize it is far lower than the average of $1,200 paid by psychiatrists" (p. 6). Turkington reveals that from 1976 to 1985, the carrier for the American Psychological Association paid out a total of $5.4 million dollars in claims, which rose to $9.7 million dollars by 1984, and to $17.2 million dollars in 1985.

Other mental health professionals (nonpsychologists) face about the same sort of conditions. For example, the policy offered to Nebraska members of the National Association of Social Work cost about $100 per year in 1987, but Florida members of the same Association were ineligible for coverage. Given the increase in liability for social workers (Besharov, 1985), it seems likely that the premium will increase for social workers and for all other health care professionals, at least for the foreseeable future.

As for other disciplines, attorneys and health care professionals alike have experienced increases. Reardon (1985) reports that a Nebraska attorney who paid about $200 for professional liability coverage in 1981, paid upwards to $2,500 in 1985; since then rates have continued to rise. Blodgett (1985) estimates "that more than 25 percent of the country's practicing lawyers do not have malpractice insurance" (p. 37), and that states are beginning to consider or implement mandatory malpractice insurance for attorneys.

As for physicians, the increasing cost of malpractice insurance is a clear-cut source of consternation, which leads to blaming "the greedy lawyers" for the malpractice "crisis." More will be said on the "crisis" shortly.

In a report on increases in malpractice insurance for physicians, Francis (1987), relying on data from the U.S. General Accounting Office, notes: For general practitioners in California, the cost of insurance has increased 173% from 1980 to 1986, with the increases for the same period being 199% for general practitioners in Florida, 335% for New York, and 239% for North Carolina. The average 1986 malpractice insurance rates for general practitioners in each of those four states respectively were $10,024, $10,448, $9,220, and $2,760. It should be noted that general practice is one of the least risky types of medical practice. For example, the 1986 rate for neurosurgeons in the same four states respectively was $37,984, $75,367, $43,019, and $18,595. Francis describes how this expense has led many physicians (especially in the high-risk specialties) to restrict or even give up their practices.

The cost of malpractice insurance is viewed by many as a necessary and reasonable business expense. In true business fashion, a health care provider passes this cost on to the health care consumers. Nonetheless, the financial impact for the professional remains.

To counter the rising cost of professional liability insurance, some state legislatures are placing restrictions on the fees that insurance companies can charge. In turn, some insurance companies are responding with a refusal to write new or amended policies. Proffer (1987) has described a new Florida restriction on insurance rates:

> The provisions in the Florida law generating the most controversy are a rollback of premium rates and other restrictions on insurance companies. Companies must give notice of cancellation well in advance, meet new standards for rate review, give rebates or credits on premiums if company profits exceed estimates, and provide new information to the insurance commissioner. The immediate 40 percent rollback of insurance premiums has drawn the most criticism, but even more is at stake. After January 1, 1987, premiums will be determined by starting with the rates applicable in 1984 and adjusting them upward or downward as justified by each insurer. (p. 270)

Proffer reveals the reactions of the insurance companies to this legislation:

> The provisions have set off a firestorm of protest from the insurers, and some threatened to withdraw from the state . . . . No companies have ceased doing business in the state, but the companies have taken a conservative approach to new business. (p. 270)

Such attitudes probably explain the previous example of a Nebraska social worker's being eligible for malpractice insurance coverage, whereas a Florida social worker would be ineligible with the same carrier. In other words, insurance carriers are combating this regulation by the

14

Florida Legislature by writing no new policies (Proffer, 1987), and some by announcing intentions to "pull out of the Florida market."

Whenever money is involved, emotions run high. The result is distrust, if not down-right paranoia, between legal and health care professionals. As McCarthy (1986) puts it:

> The malpractice issue, whether called a crisis or a breakdown, has four sides: patients, doctors, lawyers, and insurers. With immense sums of money at stake, doctors nearsightedly see lawyers as enemies and patients as potential enemies. That leaves the insurers free to raise malpractice rates to unprecedented heights. Of the three professional groups, the insurers have been making the weakest justifications for their soaring fees. (p. 2)

This cogent insight by McCarthy introduces the notion that perhaps the formulation of a "crisis" comes from other than the legalists and health care providers.

THE INSURANCE INDUSTRY

The flames of "crisis" are fanned by reports of financial losses to insurance carriers due to malpractice judgments. Unfortunately, there are conflicting definitions of what constitutes a "loss," and conflicting data on the amounts actually paid as judgments from lawsuits.

The first accusatory finger is pointed at the "ambulance chasing, shyster lawyers." This allegation is tinged with the feeling that attorneys are taking large fees from malpractice suits. There is relatively little recognition given to the facts that: (a) attorneys have strict rules imposed, typically by the supreme court of the state, about how to obtain, handle, and finance cases of this nature; (b) the cases are brought to the attorneys and courts by persons (plaintiffs) who believe they have been injured and are entitled to damages; and (c) the judgments are determined, not by the lawyers and seldom by judges, but by a jury of the plaintiff's and defendant's peers—everyday folks chosen by a jury system endorsed by public policy and established by law.

A medical source caption proclaims "Malpractice Losses Are Building—Again" (Richards, 1984), and states: "After the number of million-dollar verdicts climbed into the teens later in the 1970s, it soared to 50 in 1981 and held at 45 in 1982" (p. 108). Structured settlements (where the insurance carrier does not pay the whole amount immediately, but basically manages an investment and parcels out payment to the plaintiff over the years) are evaluated: "If these jury awards are not cause enough for wonder, the potential size of recent out-of-court, structured settlements stuns the mind" (p. 108). Richards asserts that "most actuaries agree that malpractice losses have been growing at a 15% to 20% annual rate at least since 1979" (p. 108). Citing data from a large medical-malpractice insurer, he reports that "the average cost of incurred claims against its 1,550 insured hospitals nearly doubled between 1979 and 1983" (p. 108). It is interesting that, while the average claim size reportedly increased 56% from 1979 to 1983, there was a report in the same issue of the journal that out-patient charges generally increased by 200% to 250% over the past 4 or 5 years. In other words, assuming that the stated increased costs were correct and based on an acceptable definition of "loss," the increase in malpractice claims would not, by itself, be responsible for the greatly increased out-patient costs.

There is some doubt about an escalation in amount of large awards of damages. Turkington (1986b) notes that studies between 1962 and 1985 revealed that half of the initial jury awards were decreased after trial, with the largest damage awards being the most likely to be reduced by the largest amount. Blankenship (1986) reports that of 643 tort cases (decided between January 1985 and March 1986, in Dade County, Florida), 33 (5.14%) were for at least $1 million dollars; *however*, the study failed to find any $1 million dollar plus jury verdict actually being collected. In other words, simply getting the judgment does not mean that the money will be paid.

In response to health care providers' concern about the dollar amounts of judgments, state legislatures are creating laws that will, among other things, put health care providers (namely physicians) in a position to review potential malpractice claims and place a maximum amount—for example, a $100,000 cap—on noneconomic damages, such as pain and suffering (Richards, 1984).

For example, the Michigan Legislature has enacted "Tort Reforms" (Public Acts 175, 176, and 178), which specify (among other things): (a) if a civil action is "frivolous," the court shall award costs and fees to the prevailing party against both the nonprevailing party *and* that

16

party's attorney, which should make an attorney cautious
about taking any civil suit, and certainly a malpractice
action, that is expensive to litigate; (b) if a plaintiff
rejects what proves (after litigation) to have been a
reasonable settlement offer, the rejection will negate the
plaintiff's receiving judgment interest (a similar condition
applies to the defendant); (c) mediation will be required
before litigation; (d) a cap of $225,000 for noneconomic
damages in all medical malpractice cases (with exceptions,
such as when there has been a death, an intentional tort,
fraudulent conduct by a health care provider, and so on);
and (e) a detailed statute of limitation (Shelton, Bishop, &
Blaske, 1987). There are other aspects to this Michigan
legislation that could be relevant to a malpractice suit
against a mental health professional. Fieger (1987) provides a nationwide review of medical malpractice tort reform.

The real culprit in, or creator of, the malpractice
"crisis" may be the insurance industry. Perlman (1986)
offers an analysis:

(1) In 1985, the property and casualty industry's
net worth rose by $7.6 billion! Who else can lose
money and watch its net worth increase?
(2) The industry's stocks outperformed the market
by 100 percent in 1985, and, over the last 10 years,
the leading property and casualty stocks rose by
500 percent, more than double the increase in the
Dow Jones Industrial Average. (Investors and
shareholders are told one story, and the insureds
are told another.)
(3) The industry's fourth-quarter profits were up
an incredible 881 percent over 1984 . . . . (p. 5)

Quoting an insurance industry source as saying that the
property and casualty industry is in "a stronger capital
and surplus position" than has ever been true, Perlman
agrees with the U.S. Department of Commerce's opinion
that the "crisis" is "not a crisis at all, but overly subjective
rate-making." Noting that one large insurance company
had, in 1984, suffered its first loss since the 1906 San
Francisco earthquake, Stavro (1986) reports that the same
company "came back to earn $94 million, or $4.70 per
share, on $2.7 billion in revenues last year after raising
its insurance rates by 25% to 100%" (p. 63), and further

notes that the company is "able to earn a 16% return on equity in its malpractice business" (p. 63).

Herein may lie the crux of the matter. There is ample reason to believe that there is no crisis. In other words, public policy has not become irrational and the justice system has not run amuck. The situation may simply be that health care providers and consumers, including mental health professionals *and* their clients, have become the pawns in the greatest of capitalistic games: increasing profit for the insurance industry.

The intent is not to fix blame on the insurance industry. From a mental health perspective, it is illogical and simplistic to present the health care industry as negligent enough to single-handedly create a rash of malpractice lawsuits. Likewise, it would be illogical and simplistic to present the legal profession or justice system as unethically taking advantage of insurance companies.

The reality of the "malpractice crisis" likely reflects a touch of greed from all concerned. The axiom to be recalled is "greed destroys." It is an axiom applicable to health care providers, legalists, and insurance carriers. The destruction of greed may have unintended and far-reaching effects.

What is needed is a sane view of the malpractice situation. Proffer (1987) takes an optimistic view, noting that as insurance companies benefit from increased revenues, their additional monies for investment may promote financial stability, increased competition, and the leveling out of premium costs:

> Insurance companies have raised their premiums dramatically. As the additional revenues flow in, companies will have more money to invest. The return on those investments should help relieve the present financial pinch, and allow the companies to act a little less conservatively. With fresh resources, more competition may seep into the insurance market, and premiums may level out or even decline. (p. 272)

However, Proffer warns that the cyclical nature of the insurance industry allows for slow change, and that "it will take another decade to tell if the legislative reforms of 1986 will forestall a liability crisis in 1995" (p. 272).

Mental health professionals are familiar with the pattern of new therapy approaches evolving out of the

18

shortcomings of another approach, such as the behavior therapy versus insight-oriented therapy controversy (Woody, 1971). Such controversies are usually more emotional than rational. Be it over therapeutic schools or the malpractice crisis, blaming an opposing source accomplishes little or nothing. Rather, the practicing professional should adopt a two-fold pragmatic stance: assessing risks that are associated with malpractice; and implementing and maintaining preventive and protective risk management to avoid malpractice actions.

First, the actual risk of a liability-based action should be assessed. On this point, data are scarce. Turkington (1986b) quotes a representative of the American Psychological Association Insurance Trust as saying: "Statistically, an APA member is more likely to be involved in a medical malpractice suit—as a plaintiff—than to be on the receiving end of a malpractice action" and that the "chance of being sued is half of one percent" (p. 9). Of course this estimate is based only on data for members of the American Psychological Association, and only for members who purchased insurance from the Association's endorsed carrier. It could even be argued that perhaps psychologists who are conscientious about fulfilling professional standards would care enough to pay several hundred dollars in Association dues each year, and that psychologists who are unaffiliated with the American Psychological Association might be more at risk for malpractice charges. Therefore, the Turkington (1986b) estimate should not be generalized to other mental health professionals.

When the possibility of a complaint to an ethics committee or to a state regulatory agency (such as a licensing board) is added to the chance of being a defendant in a lawsuit, the chance of being the subject of a complaint probably increases substantially. The increased risk likely would be for those mental health professionals who are minimally or poorly trained or who exercise faulty judgment in their professional practices.

Implementing and maintaining preventive and protective risk management is an absolute prerequisite for any mental health practice, with the goal of avoiding malpractice. This book is dedicated to practical ways to manage risks and avoid malpractice in mental health services.

Chapter 2:
The Mental Health Professional in Society

A malpractice legal action is a product of public policy. Public policy refers to an amorphous composite of beliefs, values, morals, needs, preferences, and coping mechanisms that are held by members of a society. When these components are expressed or communicated, they form a press for accommodation. In American society, the press is received by, among other sources, governmental units which, in turn, devise laws, regulations, and rules that spell out intentions, expectations, or directions for public servants. Although seldom considered, *a mental health professional is a public servant.*

Before public policy obtains at the practical level of ethics, regulations, or statutory and case law, there exists a societal ideal that is believed to follow laws of nature:

> Natural law philosophers think law is ordained by nature. For them, law consists of a body of higher principles existing independently of human experience. It exists as an ideal condition that is either inherent in human nature or derived from a divine source. (Blackburn, Klayman, & Malin, 1982, p. 12)

Our society believes that it has discovered certain principles of natural law, such as what constitutes being fair and just. Presumably these principles of natural law exist for all people and are not dependent upon time or culture. Rather than plunging into an esoteric debate on philoso-

21

phy, it is sufficient to acknowledge that the practical aspects of acceptable professional practices have a fundamental premise based on natural law.

The derivation of laws, regulations, and rules comes from the beliefs and knowledge of the society about the world in which it exists. In deciding upon a belief, Kerlinger (1964) points out that the person (or society) can rely on four methods: (a) the *method of tenacity* holds firmly to the truth—"the truth that they know to be true because they hold firmly to it" (p. 6), whose validity is enhanced by frequent repetition; (b) the *method of authority* accepts an established belief based on the weight of tradition and public sanction—"a large body of facts and information taken on the basis of authority" (p. 7); (c) the *a priori method* or the *method of intuition* holds that propositions accepted by reason are superior, the idea being "that men, by free communication and intercourse, can reach the truth because their natural inclinations tend toward truth" (p. 7); and (d) the *method of science* determines beliefs by external permanency, using checks that "control and verify the scientist's activities and conclusions to the end of attaining dependable knowledge outside himself" (p. 7).

A first glance might suggest a happy marriage between the legal system and the scientific method. That is, "more dependable knowledge is attained through science because science ultimately appeals to evidence: propositions are subjected to empirical test" (p. 8). To be sure, the legal system prizes *objectivity*, but its method relies on knowledge gleaned from sources other than the scientific method.

The methods of knowing have great importance for functioning as a mental health professional in our society. The scientist-practitioner model that underlies most mental health services seeks to obtain knowledge by the method of *science*. On the other hand, the nature of the legal system is probably determined least by the scientific method. It is far more reliant upon the methods of *tenacity, authority*, and *a priori* for knowing or fixing a belief. Consequently, a two-fold problem results for the mental health professional.

First, the mental health professional aspires to define "evidence" by validating and procedural forms of data (Rychlak, 1968). Validating data are gained through experiments, whereas procedural data are gained through observations, assessments, and interpretations. Both of these methods strive for replicability and control, which would allow the mental health professional to transform *personal* opinion into *professional* clinical judgment or even statistical prediction (Bartol, 1983). Reliance on professional knowledge and clinical judgment, whether in giving testimony in court or deciding upon what technique to apply to a client, differentiates the professional from the layperson.

Second, the mental health professional expects that when he or she is thrust into the legal system, whether as an expert or as a party litigant, there will be objectivity consonant with the values and standards of behavioral science. To the professional's dismay, the legal system does not hold to the scientific method. Cries of "that's wrong" or "it's unfair" are often sounded by mental health professionals embroiled in a disciplinary or legal proceeding—not because there is discrimination or unequal treatment under the law, but because the mode of operation of the legal system does not hold to the scientific method.

At a more practical level, it is well documented that the contemporary legal system is overloaded. From a survey exploring public attitudes toward attorneys and the legal system, the Florida Bar (1987) found that 80% of their sample believed that the state's court system was overworked. Marvell and Dempsey (1985) analyzed the growth of judgeships from 1970 to 1984, and found that the number of judges (nationally) increased by more than twice the population growth, but it was still far less than the caseload growth rate.

Efficiency and the scientific method, as revered by mental health professionals, do not receive a pledge of allegiance from the legal system. Bartol (1983) states:

> Note, though that a judicial system that operates in an organized, sequential, and coordinated manner between law enforcement, the courts, corrections, and probation and parole does not exist. The "system," realistically, is heavily plagued with disorganization, conflict, ambiguity, dilemma, and prejudice, and a deep-seated disenchantment emanates from all its segments. We use the word *system* only as a general term encompassing many facets; it is not meant to imply that there exists a smooth-running entity surrounded by continuity or logical processes. (pp. 10-11)

23

Bartol may be overly harsh on the legal system, but the point is well taken. The idealism and perfectionism that are endemic to the scientific method are not always present in the legal system.

By definition of professionalism, the mental health professional likely senses estrangement from this less-than-perfect legal "system." At the same time—and this is a critical principle of public policy—with all of its flaws, the existing legal system is what our society has accepted.

Every citizen is obligated to try to improve our legal system, such as by expressing opinions to our designated governmental officials. Certainly every mental health professional, by virtue of having received advanced education and accepted the endowed status of being a professional, is obligated to actively pursue improvement for all social systems. Unfortunately, it is not a perfect world.

HEALTH POLICY

Society's priorities for health services are constantly shifting. This lack of constancy can be a source of frustration to the health care professional. Accepting that society does not maintain a fixed commitment to the importance of health services has personal relevance to the professional, because it means that he or she must make adaptations in services according to the vicissitudes of health policy.

For the mental health professional who wishes to maintain practices that are safely aligned with public policy, a first order of business must be to: (a) understand and appreciate society's health policy; and (b) seek to develop an appropriate and optimum health policy for our society. Understanding and appreciating the current health policy necessitates having an open mind (relatively free from egocentric interests), whereas developing an appropriate and optimum health policy is dependent upon a willingness to promote change (often more easily said than done with some professionals) (Woody, 1985b).

When the amorphous public policy addresses a distinct issue, such as health care, a more concrete definition emerges. Thus, a policy becomes "a purposive course of action, followed by an actor or a set of actors in dealing with a problem or matter of concern" (Anderson, 1979, p. 3). In the case of health services, it means that society has transmitted through many channels a message about what it needs and how its needs should be met. The course of action prescribes a certain set of health service conditions, and the actors are the health care professionals.

It is tempting to assert that the professionals should write the script for health care. In keeping with the metaphor of the stage, society demands that it be the producer and director, who will, in turn, listen to the ideas of the actors, and will allow the script to be tailored accordingly.

AuClaire (1984) points out that the public has ambivalent attitudes about any "welfare" service, and health service is no exception. As a member of a complex society, no person can obtain, nor can any professional provide, a health service free from the dictates, priorities, and restraints imposed by public policy. Consequently, every person's health and every health care professional's practice are under the controlling influence of society.

The financing of health care is a major source of consternation for the patient, the professional, and the society. Mechanic (1981) comments:

> The psychology of illness, and the importance that consumers give to their own medical care, make policy formulation particularly difficult . . . . There is agreement that frivolous utilization and expenditures should be discouraged, but few patients ever think their own problems frivolous or unworthy of the best care available. (p. 82)

Everyone wants the best health care service possible, but there is reluctance to make the sacrifice, such as through payment of taxes, to finance health care at an optimum level.

The ambivalent views about health care lead to an unfortunate attitude of "me-ism," as opposed to "we-ism." The individual often attempts to maneuver optimum personal health care, while opposing the provision of health care services at the same level for others—particularly if the "others" are in a disenfranchised group, such as the poor.

Referring back to earlier comments, if there were ever a "natural law" for American society, it would seem to be: *costs should be minimized but service should be maximized.* This financial axiom is the source of many legal actions. Since health care is crucial for existence, it may

25

well be that finances take on a peerless status in the litigious mind.

Just as the American legal system is not perfect, the American health care system has much room for improvement. This is especially true for community-based mental health services.

All to often, it appears that our society is uncaring about the chronically ill, especially those who no longer have an obvious patient status. Mental health provides an infamous example. Based on the Mental Health Study Act (Public Law 84-142), the Joint Commission on Mental Illness and Health (1961) set into motion the most comprehensive mental health care system ever devised. On October 31, 1963, President John F. Kennedy signed into law the Community Mental Health Centers Act, and Hobbs (1964) proclaimed that our society was having a mental health revolution. Like so many revolutions, it was short-lived.

After the "Great Society" years of President Lyndon B. Johnson, a change of political support—influenced by the conflicts about the Vietnam War, the Watergate mentality, runaway inflation, and dubious governmental leadership—led to profound cutbacks in funding for mental health. Today there is only an infinitesimal commitment to community mental health. For example, the number of homeless in America is estimated to be upwards of 3 million, and (based on a Chicago sample) about 80% of them have health problems (Rossi et al., 1987). Many of the homeless street people, in another era, would probably have been treated as patients by our society. Harshbarger and Demone (1982) assert that "funds have not adequately followed clients into the community" (p. 236), and "our assumption that the principal resources for improving the quality of life for the poor would continue to rest in the public sector may no longer be tenable" (p. 237).

The mental health professional should be aware of today's cost containment dictum. Fein (1981) believes that the problems are complex and that idealism is dead. He says, "The call is for hard heads, not soft hearts, and, in the view of many, these are mutually exclusive organs of the body politic" (p. 32). Bice (1981) viewed the 1960s as a "watershed" period for health services, and considered the 1970s a period involving much more governmental regulation.

The 1980s seem to witness a societal demand for accountability. As the 1990s loom on the horizon, the futurist would probably forecast a continued lessening of fiscal support (taxation is anything but the darling of politicians, regardless of political party) and even more stringent demands being placed on the health care professional. The idealism of the 1960s that spawned health care as a right is not likely to be revived. The battle cry today is for societal accountability in contrast to the 1960s' "watershed" era of health services and the 1970s' emphasis on governmental regulation. The outlook for the 1990s points to continued lessening of financial support.

Why the escalation in liability for mental health professionals? It may be due, at least in part, to the fact that the humanitarian, publicly supported framework for health care—including mental health—services has been replaced by a commercial framework.

In the past, society thought of health care as its responsibility, and health care providers as benevolent public servants deserving of protection. Due to financial conditions, times have changed these views.

Today society is unwilling to accept responsibility for funding high-quality health care. To shift the burden, public policy considers the health care professional to be an entrepreneur. Since the entrepreneur stands to reap the financial harvest, society reasons that the health care professional must be monitored and made to pay the consequences for lapses in quality performance. In turn, the individual patient contributes to the mandate for accountability. Since the payments come directly out of the patient's pocket, instead of indirectly out of tax dollars, there is a more acute personal awareness of "getting what I pay for!"

PROFESSIONALISM IN SOCIETY

Public policy holds that our society shall have "professionals." Far too many professionals of every ilk, including those in mental health, have a tendency to believe that once they have "paid their dues" by completing university degrees, passing licensure examinations, and maintaining affiliations with professional societies, they have been ordained with a life-long right to be robed in the garments of professionalism. Such is not the case, and notions of entitlement may be a harbinger of exposure to ethical, regulatory, and legal actions.

A prerequisite for professionalism is acceptance of the fact that *there is no inalienable right to professional status.* Stated differently, *professionalism is a privilege.* Initially, the privilege must be earned and it can be continued only through fulfilling prescriptions and adhering to proscriptions set forth through public policy.

Professionalism carries a heavy burden of responsibility. The responsibility contains many duties. Failure to fulfill the responsibility and the concomitant duties constitutes the basis for complaints to ethical committees, regulatory agencies, and courts of law. As many professionals, politicians, and persons with delusions of self-importance have found out the hard way: *Regardless of station in life, no one is above the law in our American society.*

To qualify as a professional, our society requires that the person possess a unique body of knowledge. As Starkman (1978) puts it:

> The body of knowledge is entrusted to members of the occupation as guardians in terms of the generation of new knowledge, as conveyers of existing knowledge to occupational candidates, and as service users of occupational knowledge. Guardianship reflects control over use of knowledge (code) in areas that are of concern to large segments of society. Specific elements of knowledge may be used by those outside the reference group, but always under the supervision and control of members of the occupation who hold social sanction as guardians of the knowledge. (p. 58)

With mental health professionals, the required knowledge is the science of human behavior.

Society ultimately arrives at criteria of professionalism, and these may not be what the professional prefers. In the following set of criteria for professionalism, note the degree of self-determination or autonomy assigned to the professional. Following the criteria, the discussion will detail how society is less tolerant of self-determination or autonomy today than in times past.

According to Starkman (1978), the criteria for professionalism include:

1. Members possess a body of knowledge related to and essential for the role and tasks preempted. Skills that stem from the body of knowledge are of secondary importance.
2. Members are prepared to make judgments in their role and to take appropriate action when necessary, based upon their possession of the specified body of knowledge.
3. Decisions and actions are based upon knowledge related to the problem presented rather than to placate the client.
4. Members are responsible for the consequences of their judgments and actions and therefore must assume guardianship of the underlying knowledge as it relates [sic] such judgments. No one can or should tell a member how and when to use his knowledge, and "Buck Passing" stops with him.
5. In their role, members place primary emphasis on service to society.
6. Members work with colleagues to develop and enforce standards that are basic requirements for continuous improvement of their profession and in their personal practice observe such standards as are incorporated in a code of ethics that provides behavioral guides in their interactions with persons not members of the occupation.
7. Members engage in continuing search for new knowledge.
8. The services offered relate to problems of such import that high emotional involvement by recipients is a frequent concommitant [sic] of such services.
9. Outcomes of services frequently are vague and ill-defined, which results in evaluation of members' performance by peers on the basis of ritualistic behavior rather than by recipients on the basis of outcome.
10. Most members practice their profession full-time.
11. Entrants into professionalized occupations are placed under strong controls with regard to occupational socialization, with special emphasis on the development of a "professional conscience."

12. Work organization includes frequent peer contact and an elaborate technical language, as well as strong collegial ties.
13. The work organization also includes a strong voice in the determination of the circumstances under which a member functions, and typically the work organization is arranged to meet the standards of the occupation rather than extrinsic criteria.
14. Sources of income in the traditional professions are diversified to avoid conflict between professional judgments and economic security. (pp. 61-62)

These criteria reflect what the professional wishes to advocate. Today's society casts restrictions on the self-determination and autonomy interwoven throughout the criteria.

Part of the responsibility that accompanies professionalism is the ability to use the knowledge properly. Public policy today seems to doubt that health care professionals have fulfilled their duty to maintain effective self-regulatory practices. This is in contrast to, say, the 1950s and 1960s, when there was seldom a legal action against a mental health professional and almost every complaint was handled as an ethical matter. Public policy is no longer that generous today, reflecting a radical shift in the autonomy allowed to professionals. Professionals must account more to non- or extra-professional sources today than would have been true a couple of decades ago. For example, two decades ago Etzioni (1969) offered a view about professionalism that is clearly outdated:

Even the application of knowledge is basically an individual act, at least in the sense that the individual professional has the ultimate responsibility for his professional decision. The surgeon has to decide whether or not to operate. Students of the professions have pointed out that the autonomy granted to professionals who are basically responsible to their conscience (though they may be censured by their peers and in extreme cases by the courts) is necessary for effective professional work. Only if immune from ordinary social pressures and free to innovate, to experiment, to take risks without the usual social repercussions of failure, can a professional carry out his work effectively . . . . (p. x)

Although Etzioni's view may be sound in social theory, public policy has declined to allow the mental health practitioner to be "immune from ordinary social pressures and free to innovate, to experiment, to take risks without the usual social repercussions of failure." This lessened level of autonomy is evidenced by malpractice suits that assert that all treatments should meet a prudent and reasonable standard of care. Indeed, this radical shift in the amount of self-determination and autonomy is what leads many professionals to believe that there is a liability crisis.

MENTAL HEALTH SERVICE AS A BUSINESS

With the demise of the community mental health movement, the diminishing public policy priority for mental health services, the decrease in professional self-determination and autonomy, and the increase in governmental and legal monitoring of mental health practices, the contemporary mental health professional must recognize that the humanitarian, human-service model has been denigrated. Instead, public policy has created a commercial-business model for mental health practice. This is evidenced by the ever-increasing number of psychologists, psychiatrists, social workers, marriage and family therapists, mental health counselors, and the like entering into private practice and entrepreneurship, and by the entry into mental health services of health care corporations and conglomerates.

As the mental health professions have become defined, refined, and endorsed by society, the accoutrements of success (status, income, responsibility, opportunity) have followed. Competition between mental health practitioners is commonplace. This has fostered concern about proper business ethics (which may or may not be consonant with professional ethics) and governmental controls.

As societal commitment to mental health services declines, public policy inevitably changes. Bowen and Jeffers (1971) posit four directions it might take:

1. Turning the industry or large parts of it over to private enterprise.

2. Subjecting it to increased governmental controls along the lines of public utility regulation.
3. Using conditioned grants from the federal government as a means of bringing about control and reform.
4. Making it a publicly operated industry. (pp. 22 & 23)

While mental health has not become a publicly operated industry, Bowen and Jeffers were prophetic about conditioned grants from the federal government (under the Reagan administration, preference was given to block grants of federal money to a state), increased governmental controls (such as licensing and regulation of services), and an upsurge in private enterprise.

In a provocative treatise titled *The Mental Health Industry*, Magaro, Gripp, and McDowell (1978) trace the development of mental health services and propose that mental health treatment should be a "free-enterprise system." If he or she received public support, the therapist would have accountability for quality. They assert: "Public mental health clients can be made powerful consumers by rewarding practitioners for their successes rather than for their mere presence" (p. 217), much like a token economy procedure (only it would be the therapist, not the client, who was rewarded). Magaro, Gripp, and McDowell present a simple advocacy: "We are urging a return of competitive capitalism in the mental health industry" (p. 218). One might argue that the escalation of liability has fulfilled the prognosis from Magaro, Gripp, and McDowell—support, public or private, is definitely linked to accountability for quality.

Mental health services are part of the huge health care industry. Saywell and McHugh (1986) report that in 1981, 5.6 million persons were employed in health care, and in 1982, health care expenditures totaled $322.4 billion dollars (which averaged $1,365 per person, and was 10.5% of the gross national product).

As mental health services have become an integral part of the American health care system, these services have acquired acceptance and status. Mental health professionals have benefited from being a part of the larger health care "family," but they must also accept the risks associated with success and status—increased exposure and vulnerability to liability (Fisher, 1985). This book aims to prepare the professional to avoid malpractice in light of the reality that *mental health service is a business.*

A PRACTICAL GUIDE TO THE LEGAL SYSTEM

To understand the legal principles that are contained in this book, it is essential to have a basic knowledge of the legal system. (More thorough coverage is provided in Woody, 1984.) This section will present only the most important points.

Perhaps as one of the last vestiges of the now out-dated humanitarian, human-service model for mental health services, some professionals believe that legal proceedings should track much like therapeutic proceedings. Slovenko (1973) clarifies the distinctions between legal and scientific inquiries:

1. A lawsuit is not an abstract search for truth, but a proceeding to settle a controversy . . . . The court does not entertain moot controversies. (p. 8)
2. The fact-finding processes of science and of law differ in methods used to secure and test data. The scientist selects facts with a view to supporting or testing hypotheses. In law, evidence is gathered by mutually antagonistic parties. The lawyers are involved as partisans interested in the outcome of the case. Loyalty to client comes before loyalty to truth. (p. 8)
3. The legal system's method of screening data—the rules of evidence—was developed and persists for reasons that pertain uniquely to the legal craft. Under the adversary system the trial judge considers only those objections which the attorneys urge; he is not required to search for other objections which have not been asserted. (p. 8)
4. Much evidence may be rejected in a court of law, even though in other disciplines it is considered substantial enough from which to draw inferences. (p. 8)
5. A defendant is entitled to a fair trial but not a perfect one. (p. 9)
6. The law's method of arriving at a result is often purposely nonscientific or dependent upon a nonprofessional assessment. (p. 9)

33

7. Science is not concerned with values, but only with formal relationships between observable events. Results in science are based on measurement and are obtained mathematically. Results in law, on the other hand, are influenced but not ruled by hard data or hard facts. Scientific evidence, no matter how reliable, is not conclusive and binding on the court. Justice incorporates social needs as well as scientific accuracy, but neither to the exclusion of the other. (p. 9)

8. The element of subjectivity is vastly greater in law or psychiatry than in the natural sciences . . . . (p. 10)

9. Procedure—which is basically a form of Emily Post etiquette—is more important in law than in science. The content or substantive issues of the law are often resolved indirectly via questions of procedure. (p. 10)

10. One golden rule of advocacy is, "Never ask a question unless you know the answer." (p. 11)

11. A trial is basically a tribal ceremony. (p. 11)

To elaborate on Slovenko's fifth point (entitlement to a fair, but not perfect trial), an esteemed legalist on evidence said:

> A scientist can wait till he finds the data he wants; and he can use past, present, and future data; and he can go anywhere to get them . . . . But a judicial trial must be held at a fixed time and place, and the decision must be then made, once for all. (Wigmore, 1935, pp. 10-11)

From the point of view of a behavior scientist, it is easy to recognize how a mental health professional might feel uncomfortable with the ground rules for a legal proceeding.

There are two sources of law: *legislative* or *statutory* law (which would include acts, statutes, and ordinances) and *case* or *common* law (also known as judge-made law, that emanates from rulings in particular cases). Assuming an applicable jurisdiction, a statutory law prevails over a case law.

Case law is used to determine the interpretation of statutory law. Of extreme importance: (a) while there is a body of federal law that is applied to federal cases, there are circumstances that lead to the law of a state being applied even in a federal court; and (b) each state has its unique set of laws, which may or may not be compatible with the laws of another state.

Legislation and common law for a given state are usually determinative for questions of law in that state, but (again) certain circumstances can trigger looking to the laws of other states. For example, the Eighth Federal Judicial Circuit includes the states of North Dakota, South Dakota, Minnesota, Nebraska, Iowa, Missouri, and Arkansas. If a malpractice case on, say, duty to warn were being heard in a Federal Court sitting in Nebraska and there had been a case on point in, say, North Dakota Federal Court, the latter's ruling might be relied upon in precedent fashion (this example was an actuality).

Cases are typically dichotomized as *criminal* (including treason, felonies, misdemeanors) and *civil* (including contracts, domestic, torts, and others). Halfway between criminal and civil is *juvenile* law, usually for youth up to about age 18 who violate the law or need assistance or protection. Juvenile law is not the same as criminal law; it is not intended to assign punishment, but to attain rehabilitation for the youth. All cases must be conducted in accordance with the *rules of evidence* that apply to the particular court. Of most concern to the topic of risk management and avoiding malpractice are the areas of: (a) statutory laws for professional licensure (along with board-created regulations and rulings), evidence, and client's rights; and (b) case or common law pertaining to special duties and standard of care.

The federal judicial system has 94 United States District Courts. Federal courts are appropriate when, among other circumstances, there is a constitutional question, one of the parties is the federal government (such as a Veteran's Administration Hospital), one state sues another state, or there is diversity of citizenship between the parties (i.e., they live in different states and no one state can assert jurisdiction). A federal District Court case can be appealed to one of the 11 circuits of the United States Court of Appeals. There are strict rules for whether or not a case can be appealed (regardless of which court it is in), and it is usually more easily said than done. A select few cases may be appealed to the ultimate United States Supreme Court. There are also numerous specialty courts, such as the United States Tax Court.

States vary in the structure for their judicial systems. For example, Nebraska has a two-tier system, that is, district court and supreme court, whereas Florida has a three-tier system, that is, circuit court, district court of appeal, and supreme court. Each of these states also has a county court to hear certain types of cases.

Jurisdiction is a critical concept; it refers to the authority of a court to decide a particular legal question. There must be jurisdiction over the subject matter (the type of case) and the person. Within a given geographical area, a malpractice case could be heard in a federal court if one of the parties was, say, an employee of a federal hospital, clinic, or prison; or it could be heard in a state trial court. While a divorce or custody matter might be heard in a state trial court, a legal question about which state should have jurisdiction over a custody determination might belong in the federal court, if the parents lived in separate states and neither state would accept or deny jurisdiction. A debt of a few hundred dollars (say, what a patient owes to a mental health professional for services) might be heard in the small claims court. If the amount were larger, it might fall under the jurisdiction of the county court. If it reached a still higher amount, the district or circuit trial court might have jurisdiction. The exact title and jurisdiction of the court depends upon the state's statutes. A more detailed discussion of this matter is provided by Woody and Mitchell (1984).

The *rules of evidence* deserve special mention. They control what will and will not be admitted into evidence. Many of the suggestions for avoiding malpractice set forth in this book were formulated with the rules of evidence in mind. For example, the hearsay rule typically precludes testimony by someone who was not present at the occurrence of the event in question. There are, however, exceptions to the hearsay rule which allow: "A statement of the declarant's then existing state of mind, emotion or physical sensation . . ." (Florida Statutes, 90.803(3)(a), 1985); or "Statements made for purposes of medical diagnosis or treatment . . ." (Florida Statutes 90.803(4), 1985); or "A memorandum, report, record or data compilation . . ." (Florida Statutes 90.803(6)(a), 1985). Each of these and other exceptions to the hearsay rule potentially allow the mental health professional to bring in testimony from a colleague with whom he or she had shared case information for supervisory goals, and thereby establish, for example, that a reasonable standard of care had been maintained. A reminder: The rules of evidence are highly similar among the states, but there are unique factors (the previous Florida rules may or may not be the same as the rules for another state).

Also highly important in avoiding malpractice, every mental health practitioner should have a basic understanding of *tort* law. Many of the causes of action, as delineated in Chapter 1, come from tort law.

A *tort* is a civil wrong. Some acts that are torts (such as assault) may also be prosecuted criminally. A tort occurs when a person by commission (act) or omission (failing to act when there is a duty) causes another person to suffer injury to person, property, or recognized interest (Kionka, 1977). Among other possibilities: Injury to a person could be infliction of mental distress; injury to property could be destruction of a possession; and injury to a recognized interest could be interference with business.

In any tort case, the injury must be compensable; the court must be able to assess the value of the damage, to provide a remedy to the injured party.

Torts can have either an *intentional* or a *negligence* basis. Chapter 3 will cover the legal theory for negligence, the criteria that must be satisfied to establish the cause of action, and the nature and types of legal remedies. For now, brief descriptions of intentional and negligence torts are in order.

To establish an intentional tort, the *prima facie* case must provide three elements of proof: (a) an act, (b) an intention, and (c) an injury. Intentional torts include: *battery* (harmful or offensive contact with the person); *assault* (causing reasonable apprehension of an immediate, harmful, or offensive contact with a person); *false imprisonment* (confining a person to a specific, bounded area); and *intentional infliction of mental distress* (acting in an extreme and outrageous behavior that transcends the decency tolerated by society). There are also other intentional torts (e.g., defamation of character or invasion of privacy) (Palagi & Springer, 1984).

Negligence is based on the premise of a person's having a duty to someone else, failing to fulfill that duty, and being the cause of an injury with a compensable outcome. For mental health professionals, the four-step negligence sequence is applied to a *standard of care*. That is, negligence occurs if the mental health professional breaches an acceptable standard of care and such ↳.each causes the patient to have compensable injuries.

Some commissions or omissions of acts can lead to multiple torts, and a lawsuit against a defendant could allege several counts. For example, consider a therapist who confines the client to an isolation room, persists in physical contact (e.g., shaking the client), and verbally creates extreme emotional arousal—in the name of "action-oriented therapy." If the client later files a legal action against the therapist, it might allege battery, assault, false imprisonment, intentional infliction of mental distress, and probably other allegations. The therapist would have to establish that the procedures were in accord with what a reasonable and prudent therapist would practice. This example is more complex legally than the basic issue of standard of care, but it is sufficient to illustrate how multiple counts can enter into a legal action against a mental health professional.

There can, of course, be other types of legal actions against a mental health professional. Under contract law, for example, there could be a dispute about: (a) whether the landlord or the therapist should pay for remodeling the therapist's suite of offices; (b) the conditions for the services that the therapist was to have provided to a hospital; or (c) the results that the client could have reasonably expected to receive, based on the agreed-upon treatment plan. Product liability law could be applied to hold the therapist responsible for injuries caused by defective therapy apparatus (which could have been defective in design and/or usage) (Schutz, 1982). A wrongful death action, in which a person's death is attributed to the omissions or commissions of the professional(s), can also be brought to the court. In mental health services, this action is exemplified by allegations that the mental health professionals who served a client should have done more to predict and prevent his or her suicide. The list of types of legal action that could be filed against a mental health professional could go on and on.

PERSONAL CONSIDERATIONS

From serving as legal counsel to mental health professionals faced with ethical, regulatory, or legal actions, I have witnessed how being named a defendant touches the very core of personal and professional identity. It is axiomatic that the professional person's career constitutes a primary definition of one's sense of self-worth. For the mental health professional, the career choice may deeply influence personal identity.

By entering the field of human services, the mental health professional acknowledges, internally and externally, a life purpose of supporting human welfare, and judges self-worth accordingly to achieving this purpose. When a disconsolate client attacks the ethical or legal functioning of the mental health practitioner, even the seasoned professional will struggle with devastatingly negative emotional reactions.

Sometimes the old adage, "I have met the enemy, and it is I," holds true for mental health professionals under ethical or legal fire. Wright (1981) quotes an attorney-friend as saying about therapists faced with legal actions:

> Heaven protect me from intelligent, sophisticated clients. While they're "helping" me win my case, they can find ways I never dreamed of to mess things up. The smarter they are the more ways they can find to botch it. (p. 1535)

Being intelligent, a mental health professional is likely to resent such an accusation, but the comment is lamentably true. The mental health professional must remember that the courtroom is not a therapy room (reflect back to the quotations from Slovenko). As Wright, a psychologist, interprets the foregoing view from the attorney:

> I think the attorney was recognizing that the psychologist's professional training, experience, and life-style ill equips us to defend ourselves and may tend to make us more vulnerable to the aggressive maneuverings of the plaintiff's advocate. Our training and our personal philosophies tend to emphasize the importance of the individual and our obligation as a helper/practitioner to evidence humanistic concerns or attempt "conflict resolution." We find it hard to believe that our virtue is unappreciated, so we attempt to follow our ethical admonitions to resolve conflict and discover to our subsequent dismay that the plaintiff's attorney made our virtuous and well-meaning efforts appear to be an attempt to "cover up" or "cop out." (p. 1535)

Wright recognizes that mental health professionals hold a philosophical stance that can be self-defeating in an adversarial encounter.

During therapy, attempts to reconcile differences between the client and the therapist can be productive and constructive. During a legal action, it is a different story. When the therapist attempts to reconcile differences directly with a party-opponent (or his or her legal advocate), the tactic that was productive and constructive in therapy can suddenly become unproductive and destructive.

The message is simple: When faced with a disconsolate client, forget trying to be a therapist. In almost every instance, the therapist's duty to the client has been eliminated by the client's resorting to litigation. Instead, the prudent mental health professional should decisively seek the support and expertise of an attorney.

Professionalism is coveted, yet it can be a source of personal vulnerability: "The greater the degree of professionalism one demands of oneself, the more detailed and excruciating is the attendant review and the more intense the accompanying feelings of threat, anxiety, guilt, remorse, and depression" (Wright, 1981, p. 1535).

This relationship between the degree of professionalism and emotional response is exemplified by the mental health professional who was facing a complaint filed with a state department of licensing. Upon learning of the complaint, she lamented, "To think, I had entertained the idea of trying to get appointed to the state board, and now the board is after me—there goes my chance of ever being affiliated with the licensing process." This poignant comment reveals more than the person's dismay. It reveals the professional's vulnerability—that one with impeccable credentials and an outstanding career record, who was justly considering the possibility of becoming part of the collective conscience of the profession, could be assailed by an accusatory former client, for apparently no reason other than the client's pathological vindictiveness.

Being named in a legal action is something that can happen to any mental health professional. Clearly, there are safeguards against a negative outcome, such as advanced training, steadfast adherence to professional ethics, and consistent exercise of prudence and reason in service, but neither these nor any other precaution can completely insulate the mental health professional from an attack. Given the escalation of litigation, whatever be the form or forum, and the pathological or characterlogic nature of clients, there is no escaping the possibility of malpractice complaint.

With this reality to face, the provider of mental health services needs a logical framework for practice that encompasses risk management to avoid malpractice. This book offers information, guidance, and many practical suggestions that will gird the mental health professional with protective armour.

What is needed first and foremost is a new cognitive set. The realistic view is that *a legal complaint is possible against the best of practitioners.* If and when a complaint occurs, it should not be interpreted as a pre-ordained judgment of professional competence or self-worth. In today's mental health services, litigation goes with the territory. Every contemporary mental health professional has to be armed personally and professionally to cope with and counter the assault.

One attitude that will be useful is to recognize that *the complaint is coming from one client,* and that *faulty perceptions and judgments are sometimes to be expected of persons seeking mental health treatment.* Under our American legal system, everyone—and most certainly a client—has a right to pursue a remedy for a perceived wrong. This does not, however, mean that all perceived wrongs are based on reality.

Instead of an attitude of paranoid disbelief in the alleged complaint, it is reasonable to have faith that the legal system will allow a fair and just process for the mental health professional's rights as well as for the client's rights. In fact, there seems to be a tendency for the legal system to strain to give the defendant-professional the benefit of the doubt, unless the proof is to the contrary.

A second useful attitude is to expend appropriate emotional energy, but not "catastrophize" the legal problem. There is apt to be confusion, self-doubt, and emotional turmoil and pain. When these conditions plague the mind, the mental health professional needs to accept the challenge to "practice what you preach." Ironically, one therapist who specialized in cognitive restructuring told of how he was impaired by recurring thoughts, to the point of near obsession, about a legal case against him. It is necessary to counter irrational, destructive, obsessive reactions with logical and planned efforts of defense.

Keeping anxiety under control is made difficult by the fact that legal cases are seldom over quickly. The wheels of justice turn slowly; even the most mundane legal issues can drag on and on. With a rational cognitive set, the mental health professional can cope and endure. Optimum legal strategy requires that the professional control his or her emotions to avoid self-defeating responses.

As with all crises, life must go on even in the midst of pain and confusion; the embattled mental health professional must continue throughout the pending litigation with business as usual. Litigation is a public matter, and the professional should expect that the gossipy nature of people, including professional colleagues, will bring the matter to the attention of others. Personal and professional relationships may indeed be strained, even to the point of no more referrals from sources who adopt a "wait-and-see" approach to the litigation.

The practitioner must recognize that litigation is, regrettably, an ingredient of today's commercial framework for mental health services. Just as funds are allocated for equipment, furnishings, books and journals, supplies, advertising, secretarial assistance, and organizational memberships, the mental health professional should *conceptualize costs of preventive and defensive measures as necessary business expenses.*

It is interesting that a therapist has no hesitation, and rightly so, in charging a treatment fee for his or her services, but is commonly reluctant to incur expenses from seeking legal counsel, as well as other professional guidance. It is illogical to expect to conduct an efficient, prosperous, and legally safe mental health practice today without regular inputs from, at least, an attorney and an accountant. This era mandates preventive and defensive measures to develop, maintain, and safeguard the business and financial dimensions of mental health services.

Chapter 3:
Negligence
and Standard of Care

By definition, "professional malpractice" means that the practitioner has failed to uphold a standard of care that has been endorsed by his or her discipline. The failure is assessed according to negligence theory.

Endorsement by one's colleagues is not adequate to justify professional functioning. When a group of professionals is in general agreement about what should or should not be done in serving clients and they function accordingly, this consensual framework is considered to establish the "customary" or "community practice" standard. A customary or community practice is subject to further ratification, namely by public policy.

Through its courts, public policy holds that a community practice may fail to be adequate: "Even an entire industry, by adopting such careless methods to save time, effort or money cannot be permitted to set its own uncontrolled standard" (Keeton et al., 1984, p. 194).

Basically, the public-policy test involves evaluating what benefits would be derived from a certain practice and how expensive it would be to administer it. The expense is determined by the amount of professional and client time, the costs involved, and the risks incurred.

An example in mental health malpractice would be the prediction of dangerousness. Legally, a practitioner has a duty to warn of dangerousness and, depending upon the circumstances, a duty to protect the client or others from violence. Research is quite clear that mental health professionals have limited ability to predict dangerousness; there will be a high percentage of the clients identified as dangerous who will, in fact, commit no violent act (i.e., false-positive predictive errors) and vice versa. Nonetheless, public policy holds that the benefits to society justify such faulty predictions, even at the risk of infringing on the civil rights of the potentially dangerous client (e.g., eliminating the right to confidentiality and privileged communication for the protection from physical harm to self or others).

Some mental health practitioners assert that their theory of intervention does not accommodate assessment of any kind. For example, certain humanistic approaches to psychotherapy would view assessment as having a negative consequence for the therapeutic processes, and resist making any assessment of dangerousness.

Some mental health practitioners may lack training in psychological testing or other formal assessment techniques. Therefore, they would assert, "it is not within our 'community practice' standard to use an assessment technique with every client."

Nonplused by professional denials, court rulings support two public policy dicta. First, *every mental health professional must have competency with some type of assessment technique for predicting dangerousness.* Second, *even if most of the practitioners in a discipline do not use an assessment technique, its cost is justified by any significant benefit that will accrue from its use in protection from physical injury for clients and society.*

The standard of care is more than locally determined. Historically, practitioners could be isolated from the mainstream of professional thought, and public policy was tolerant of sacrificing familiarity with research and optimum standards to gain clinical service where it was needed. Thus, the standard of care by which practice was deemed to be adequate or inadequate was dependent upon the locale.

Today the communication media allow for dissemination of research advances to any practitioner, and professional journals reach readers in a timely fashion, regardless of geographical location. Jet travel allows the practitioner from a remote location to obtain continuing education on virtually any subject quickly and economically.

Consequently, malpractice is now defined, in part, by national standards. There are still jurisdictions that may require establishing the community practice standard. For example, an expert brought in to testify about a national standard may need to be familiar with practice in the community; this restriction is presumably justified by the need for expert opinion to assist the court in deciding how to apply the national standard to the local scene.

A trend is for a national standard—especially if the defendant-practitioner has, in any way, held himself or herself out to the client (or the public) as having the competencies of a "specialist." "If a therapist represents himself as a specialist, he will be held to the highest standards of a specialist, even if that claim is a misrepresentation" (Schutz, 1982, p. 4).

The "specialist rule" goes beyond the explicit statements of the practitioner, such as how he or she advertises in the yellow pages of the telephone directory. It also applies if the client has a *reasonable basis for believing* that the practitioner is a specialist, as might be assumed from certificates on the wall that reflect attendance at specialized seminars, the types of literature in the waiting room, or the therapist's demeanor.

The trend toward a national standard for specialists is reflected in common law (case rulings). Moreover, statutes of some states specify the use of a national standard for specialists.

To clarify the specialist rule, purporting to be a specialist elevates the standard of care to a comparison with specialists on the particular practice topic, and a national standard is applied. This commonly means looking to the standards promulgated by a national professional organization with a focus on the specialization.

For example, if the practitioner professed to be, or the client had a reasonable basis for believing that the practitioner was, a specialist in sex therapy, the standards set forth by the American Association of Sex Educators, Counselors, and Therapists would probably be weighted heavily by the court, when considering if the therapist's actions with the client constituted acceptable professional conduct or revealed sexual misconduct. In these instances, it seldom matters if the practitioner has no affiliation with the standards-setting organization. Suggestions will be made later for avoiding an unnecessary or unwise elevation of the standard of care to the level of a specialist.

NEGLIGENCE THEORY

The underlying theory for determining malpractice is negligence. Negligence only occurs when there is liability; that is, the actor has a *duty to fulfill a standard.* Negligence is embraced by the law of torts. Each of these components shall be considered.

A *tort* is "a civil wrong wherein one person's behavior causes a compensable injury to the person, property, or recognized interest of another and which a civil remedy is sought" (Palagi & Springer, 1984, p. 155). Torts include *intentional* and *unintentional* torts. Chapter 2 provided introductory information about tort law; the subject will now be detailed.

Intentional torts are basically the civil version of criminal law. They involve an *act*, an *intention*, and an *injury.* Of concern to mental health services, causes of action relevant to an intentional tort include: *assault* (an action that is intended to and does cause reasonable apprehension of immediate, harmful, or offensive contact with a person); *battery* (a harmful or offensive contact with another person); *false imprisonment* (wrongfully confining a person to a bounded area, which has sometimes been used to refer to wrongful hospitalization of a mental patient); and *intentional infliction of mental distress* (an extreme and outrageous act that is intended to cause severe mental distress to a person).

Unintentional torts are actions, by omission or commission, that violate the elements of negligence. *Professional malpractice is the prime example of an unintentional tort.* More will be said about intentional torts in the later material on the elements of negligence.

Liability is the legal responsibility, due to an action, for a negative outcome. The esteemed legalist Oliver Wendell Holmes, Jr., clarified the fluid nature of liability in a lecture presented in 1881:

> The business of the law of torts is to fix the dividing lines between those cases in which a man is liable for harm which he has done, and those in which he is not. But it cannot enable him to predict with certainty whether a given act under given circumstances will make him liable, because an act will rarely have that effect unless followed by damage, and for the most part, if not always,

the consequences of an act are not known, but only guessed at as more or less probable. All the rules that the law can lay down beforehand are rules for determining the conduct which will be followed by liability if it is followed by harm—that is, the conduct which a man pursues at his peril. A choice which entails a concealed consequence is as to that consequence no choice. (Holmes, 1966/1881, p. 3)

As this discussion later moves into suggestions for avoiding malpractice, the preceding quote, "A choice which entails a concealed consequence is as to that consequence no choice," should serve as a reminder of the need for prudence in clinical practice.

Liability is imposed for a negative consequence, and negligence is the framework applied to determine if the liability justifies a remedy. Yale Law Professor Fleming James, Jr. (1966/1951) states: "Negligence is 'conduct which falls below the standard established by law for the protection of others against unreasonable risk of harm'" (p. 9). He points out that negligence is measured by what a (mythical) "reasonably prudent" person would do under the circumstances. The subjective version would consider the limits of the given clinician:

By and large the law has chosen external, objective standards of conduct. The reasonably prudent man is, to be sure, endowed with some of the qualities of the person whose conduct is being judged, especially where the latter has greater knowledge, skill, or the like, than people generally. But many of the actor's shortcomings, such as awkwardness, faulty perception, or poor judgment, are not taken into account if they fall below the general level of the community. This means that individuals are often held guilty of legal fault for failing to live up to a standard which as a matter of fact they cannot meet. (James, 1966/1951, p. 10)

The objective version could require meeting a standard that is beyond the actor's capacity. When considering negligence by a professional, the press from public policy is for a minimum level of knowledge and competency, and the personal shortcomings of the practitioner will receive little or no consideration in judging adherence to or violation of the standard of care for the discipline.

THE FOUR ELEMENTS OF NEGLIGENCE

Negligence is composed of four elements: (a) duty, (b) breach of duty, (c) causation, and (d) harm. Putting it in a clinical framework, Schutz (1982) describes the four elements as follows: "(1) that a therapist-patient relationship was established; (2) that the therapist's conduct fell below the acceptable standard of care; (3) that the conduct was the proximate cause of an injury to the patient; (4) that an actual injury was sustained by the patient" (p. 2).

The critical importance of negligence justifies a more detailed description, relying on legal language. A translation into the language of the mental health practitioner will follow:

Negligence is simply one kind of conduct. But a cause of action founded upon negligence, from which liability will follow, requires more than conduct. The traditional formula for the elements necessary to such a cause of action may be stated briefly as follows:

1. A duty, or obligation, recognized by the law, requiring the person to conform to a certain standard of conduct, for the protection of others against unreasonable risks.
2. A failure on the person's part to conform to the standard required: a breach of the duty. These two elements go to make up what the courts usually have called negligence; but the term quite frequently is applied to the second alone. Thus it may be said that the defendant was negligent, but is not liable because he was under no duty to the plaintiff not to be.
3. A reasonably close causal connection between the conduct and the resulting injury. This is what is commonly known as "legal cause," or "proximate cause," and which includes the notion of cause in fact.
4. Actual loss or damage resulting to the interests of another . . . . Nominal damages, to vindicate a technical right, cannot be removed in a negligence action, where no actual loss has occurred.

> The threat of future harm, not yet realized is not enough. Negligent conduct in itself is not such an interference with the interests of the world at large that there is any right to complain of it, or to be free from it, except in the case of some individual whose interests have suffered. (Keeton et al., 1984, pp. 164-165)

This definition is one of the most relevant and authoritative available to mental health practitioners, and deserves careful consideration.

Two added negligence concepts: (a) a person may not bring a lawsuit based on negligence without standing, meaning he or she is an "individual whose interests have suffered"; and (b) public policy supports that a legal action must be timely, and statutes create a "statute of limitation," restricting the time frame for bringing a legal action. On the latter, the current fluctuation caused by tort reform legislative efforts precludes a distinct guideline on statute of limitation, but generally a legal action must be filed within a given number of months from the time of the malpractice, or from the time that the injury was or should have been discovered.

Duty. In professional negligence, it is almost a foregone conclusion that the practitioner has a duty to a client. A question might arise, however, as to whether the duty extends to the client's family members or significant others.

Breach of Duty. For negligence, the conduct of the practitioner must fall short of the standard of care that is owed to the client. How the standard of care is defined will be explained shortly. For now, it should be recognized that the plaintiff-client has the burden of proof for establishing that the practitioner acted unreasonably (had breached the applicable standard of care for the mental health service) and that, because of the breach, injury actually occurred to the client.

An exception to proving that the practitioner acted unreasonably is created by the *res ipsa loquitur* principle. This principle translates into "the thing speaks for itself." It contributes to establishing negligence by showing that the injury does not ordinarily occur if the person in charge of the situation, namely the practitioner, uses ordinary care, and that the instrumentality that led to the injury was under the management and control of the defendant-practitioner.

For example, the practitioner could maintain that he or she followed acceptable procedures in using hypnotic age regression with the client, but if the client suffered actual injury (e.g., extreme mental distress from reliving a traumatic episode), the *res ipsa loquitur* principle might sustain a cause of action against the well-meaning practitioner.

Also, if there is a statute in the state that spells out a standard of care, proof that the practitioner did not fulfill the statutory prescription (an omission) or proscription (a commission) could sustain a cause of action based on negligence.

Violation of a statute may lead to *negligence per se*, which Schutz (1982) describes as follows:

> Negligence per se is the judicial rule that a violation of statute, governmental guidelines (such as the National Institute of Mental Health standards), or a court order *may* be the basis for action when (1) the injured party is a member of the class for whose benefit the statute was enacted, (2) the resultant injury is of the type contemplated by the statute, and (3) the breach is the proximate cause of the injury. The reasoning behind this rule is that statutes are formulated to be the standard of reasonable conduct and embody the experience of the entire community, which may have had the benefit of expert testimony in hearings to draft the guidelines or statutes. (p. 5)

In mental health, this statutory authority would likely be in the licensing law for the discipline or the rules promulgated by the regulatory agency (e.g., the board of examiners for licensing the discipline).

Sometimes being guilty of violating a criminal law will support a civil negligence action. For example, state criminal laws are, more and more, codifying that it is a crime for a health care provider, such as a psychotherapist, to engage in sexual activity with a client. If a practitioner is found guilty of such a crime, the victim can also be a plaintiff in a malpractice suit against the practitioner. Incidentally, being found guilty of a crime is not a prerequisite for a sexual misconduct malpractice action.

Causation. A finding of negligence requires that the conduct of the defendant be the proximate cause of the injury suffered by the plaintiff. It must be proved that the practitioner's omission or commission led to the client's injury. Typically, the "but for" test applies. The plaintiff-client alleges that "but for the conduct of the defendant-practitioner, I would not have suffered the injury."

It is feasible that the practitioner was negligent, but a superseding force intervened, breaking the causal connection between the practitioner's negligence and the client's injury. This could absolve the practitioner of liability. For example, the aforementioned hypnotic age regression may have led to a weakened ego state, but the injuries suffered were really attributable to the spouse abuse inflicted on the client when he or she returned home. Of course, if there was an ongoing history of spouse abuse, if the therapist's hypnotic intervention weakened the ego state, and if he or she did not take reasonable steps to keep the client away from the situation (known to carry a high risk of violence), the liability might still remain with the practitioner.

Injury. "Negligent conduct in itself is not such an interference with the interests of the world at large that there is any right to complain of it, or to be free from it, except in the case of some individual whose interests have suffered" (Keeton et al., 1984, p. 165). There are two messages within the above quotation: (a) The person must have been affected, thereby creating standing; and (b) "suffered" refers to being harmed or experiencing injury. Harm can include a violation of civil rights, or extend to mental and/or physical injury. Unless there is injury, there can be be no remedy.

REMEDIES

A client who takes legal action against a mental health practitioner may or may not be realistic about what to expect. Some clients who believe they have a *bona fide* legal complaint against a practitioner want revenge (such as a client whose transference-based love was unfulfilled by the therapist). Other clients profess a public-service motive: "I only want to be sure that he or she does not do such a dastardly thing to someone else." Some clients want recompense for injuries suffered (such as lowered earning capacity because of the emotional trauma due to professional negligence). In most instances, recompense is the only legitimate motive for a client.

Some would-be plaintiff-clients walk into the attorney's office with, figuratively, dollar signs in their eyes. They have heard the exaggerated stories about receiving awards of millions of dollars, but they lack an awareness of the difficulty and expense associated with gaining a judgment. Most often, the client has never considered the need to prove injury.

Punitive Damages. "Punitive or exemplary damages are awarded to punish the defendant for aggravated, willful, wanton, or outrageous acts and to deter him from similar conduct in the future" (Palagi & Springer, 1984, p. 197).

Some jurisdictions (but not all) allow punitive damages. When punitive damages are awarded by a court, it is usually for an intentional tort (such as assault and battery), not because of mere negligence. Punitive damages might also be supported by willful and malicious behavior, or conduct that shocked the conscience of the court. In these instances, the court might award punitive damages to teach a lesson to others. "In determining an award for punitive damages, a jury will consider the following elements: the character of the defendant's conduct; the seriousness of the loss or injury to the plaintiff; the defendant's financial status; and the expense of the litigation and the attorney's fee to the plaintiff" (Palagi & Springer, 1984, p. 197). Thus, if a mental health practitioner is found to have committed gross negligence, such as subjecting clients to abuse, punitive damages might be awarded to teach other practitioners never to do such a detestable act; punitive damages may also be directed at attorneys' fees.

Contrary to popular belief, punitive damages are seldom awarded in professional negligence cases, and there seems to be a trend, at least in many states, against punitive damages. However, if the conscience of the court is shocked and the jurisdiction does not allow punitive damages, the judge (through rulings of law and/or jury instructions) and the jury (through rulings of fact) have considerable leeway for elevating the amount of the award for other forms of damages.

Purpose of Damages. The basic purpose of damages in negligence cases is *compensatory.* The award of damages is not to be punitive *per se.* Public policy endorses that the plaintiff should be *restored to his or her pre-injury condition.* It is clearly impossible to shape a remedy that will truly restore the person to the pre-injury state, because merely experiencing the emotional or physical injury has a scarring effect.

General Damages. The plaintiff is entitled to a financial award that will compensate for the damages from the injury. Most commonly, general damages are awarded for pain and suffering (past, present, and future), disability (loss of mobility), loss of enjoyment of life, embarrassment or humiliation, disfigurement (loss of limb, scars), and diminished earning capacity attributable to the injury. General damages may not require proof of pecuniary loss, and may allow compensation for bodily harm and emotional distress.

Special Damages. The plaintiff is entitled to a financial recovery of all losses and expenses incurred as a result of injury. This includes medical and other health-related bills, lost wages or business profits (past, present, and future), household help, property damage, damage for unusual effects, and so on. Basically, compensation is possible for any reasonable expense due to the injury.

General and special damages may be based on expenses already incurred, or those which will be incurred in the future. Future expenses cannot be highly speculative, and expert testimony is typically necessary to justify a predicted expense.

If the plaintiff-client alleges that he or she is less able to work in the future because of an injury, such as mental distress, caused by the defendant-practitioner's negligence, an expert in relevant economic principles is needed to present an estimate of the decreased earning potential. If it is alleged that ongoing psychotherapy and/or rehabilitation is needed, a professional will have to provide a learned opinion about the duration and cost of such services.

Awards for future economic loss are commonly discounted to their present value. That is, the award will be for an amount of money that, if reasonably and safely invested, will pay off in the future the amount of economic losses that will be sustained in the long-run. An exception is that the award for future pain and suffering is usually not discounted.

Consequential Damages. Beyond the plaintiff-client, negligence can lead to loss or injury to third parties, most notably spouses, children, parents, other family members, (occasionally) employers, and (with a client who committed suicide or a person who was killed by a client because of the practitioner's negligence) an estate.

Perhaps the best-known reason for consequential damages is "loss of consortium," meaning that the injured party (say, a spouse) was deprived of love, companionship, sexual relations, material services, conjugal fellowship, and other factors associated with the loss or partial loss of a spouse (Belli, 1980). Loss of consortium is essentially a form of mental suffering that could reasonably be expected as a consequence of the injured person's state.

Nominal Damages. Sometimes an award will be for a token amount. "Nominal damages are awarded to an injured party when there is no substantial loss or injury to be compensated but, instead, merely a technical invasion of the injured party's legally protected rights" (Palagi & Springer, 1984, p. 195).

An award of nominal damages symbolizes the declaration of a right, such as that the client has a right to not be touched by the therapist. A nominal damage award also assigns the blame to the wrongdoer. If a party is "distasteful" or does not seem to "deserve" substantial compensation (e.g., a convict who sues a prison therapist), a nominal award can be made to uphold the right but deny financial benefits to a person disliked by society. A nominal award might be used to cover the "winning" party's court costs and attorney's fees. Some clients might be willing to receive a nominal award because it proves that they were right, but their attorneys might view a nominal award as a disaster because they would not receive adequate payment for their legal services.

Other Remedies. For malpractice, the primary remedy is financial compensation. Some clients, however, will want to gain satisfaction, be it for revenge or for protecting society, through other means.

A client can file a complaint with a professional ethics committee and/or a governmental regulatory agency. The latter would include the state department vested with the responsibility for enforcing the relevant statutes, such as the Department of Professional Regulation and the concomitant licensing board(s). Complaints to professional ethics committees and governmental regulatory agencies are discussed in detail elsewhere (Woody, 1988).

Many attorneys unabashedly seek to dissuade clients with a viable malpractice suit from filing an ethics or regulatory complaint—unless, of course, the results of the ethics committee or regulatory agency would assuredly complement the legal action and the award of damages.

DEFENSES

Virtually all of the practical suggestions set forth in later chapters are devoted to defense of the mental health practitioner. Many of the suggestions are, however, proactive: ways that, by early adoption, the practitioner can stave off any malpractice action. At this point, consideration can be limited to the legal defenses orchestrated by the defendant-practitioner's attorney during the course of a malpractice case.

The fundamental defense is that there was *no breach of the standard of care*. Mental health counterparts would be called upon, by affidavit and/or courtroom testimony (depending upon the stage of the litigation), to offer a professional opinion on behalf of the defendant-practitioner, asserting that his or her services to the client were reasonable and appropriate for the clinical situation.

A second defense is *lack of injury, harm, or damage*. As discussed previously, to be actionable, negligence must produce harm or damage. With the kinds of damages alleged by clients against mental health practitioners, it is commonplace to have a basis for doubt about the existence of injury or, if there is an indication of injury, the severity of the damage. The plaintiff will be obligated to provide expert testimony to establish the presence and extent of injury, and the remedy that is appropriate. It could be asserted that the damages are too speculative to justify a remedy. The defendant-practitioner must be prepared to launch a counterattack on the validity of the claims for presence and extent of injury. The counterattack must be unrestrained by any sense of altruism or nurturance for the client-turned-litigant.

A third defense, *assumption of risk*, is especially relevant to mental health services. From the onset of service, and at any time thereafter that a new or modified intervention is made, the client should be provided with information about the nature of the procedure and the risk (if any) associated with it. If the client grants informed consent, voluntarily and with knowledge, the practitioner can defend against a malpractice action by showing that the client assumed the risk. There are conditions, however, that would lead to a public-policy basis for rejecting this defense, such as the procedure's being too experimental or lacking in standards endorsed by the profession.

One special problem emerges from the fact that a client seeking services from a mental health practitioner may have a dubious state of competency. Therefore, care should be exercised to document the client's competency at the time that informed consent is granted. If the client lacks competency, a written approval from the client's guardian or conservator must be obtained.

A fourth defense is *contributory negligence*. Keeton et al. (1984) state: "Contributory negligence is conduct on the part of the plaintiff, contributing as a legal cause to the harm he has suffered, which falls below the standard to which he is required to conform for his own protection" (p. 451). Contributory negligence is akin to assumption of risk, except "the defense does not rest upon the idea that the defendant is relieved of any duty toward the plaintiff" (p. 451), only that "the plaintiff is denied recovery because his own conduct disentitles him to maintain the action" (p. 452).

In some jurisdictions, contributory negligence results in the the court's dividing the liability for the injury between the client and the practitioner, that is, proportioning the damages. This is known as the "pure approach" to *comparative negligence*. Thus, if damages were assessed to be, say, $100,000 and the client's negligence was equal to the practitioner's negligence in causative force, the practitioner would be subject to a judgment of $50,000.

Some jurisdictions hold that as long as a plaintiff's contributory negligence does not exceed a certain percentage of responsibility, say 50%, there will be no bar to his or her recovery. Other jurisdictions predicate a recovery for the plaintiff on his or her being less at fault than the defendant: "Under both systems, the plaintiff's contributory negligence operates as a complete bar, and he takes nothing, if his fault exceeds the permitted threshold amount; if his negligence falls below that amount, his damages are reduced proportionately to his fault" (Keeton et al., 1984, p. 473). These two versions are referred to as a "modified approach" to comparative negligence.

Each jurisdiction has a unique definition and interpretation of contributory and comparative negligence. Any defense must be carefully determined and developed, according to the facts of and conditions for the particular case. The mental health practitioner should be informed about defenses relevant to malpractice, but the attorney should be granted full authority for deciding on the legal defensive strategy.

STANDARD OF CARE

The breach-of-duty element in the negligence formula is determined by the standard of care that would be maintained by the reasonable and prudent practitioner under the same circumstances. The "reasonable and prudent practitioner" is a fiction.

The early definitions of standard of care were relevant to medical practice, but their principles continue to this day and "many of the legal principles governing such actions may apply with equal force to malpractice claims asserted against other health care providers" (King, 1977, p. 7).

The health care provider is not expected to be perfect, and the client is not guaranteed a result—only that certain standards will be maintained in treatment:

[The medical professional] does not warrant or insure the outcome of his treatment, and he will not be liable for an honest mistake of judgment, where the proper course is open to reasonable doubt. But by undertaking to render medical services, even though gratuitously, he will ordinarily be understood to hold himself out as having standard professional skill and knowledge. The formula under which this usually is put to the jury is that he must have the skill and learning commonly possessed by members of the profession in good standing; and he will be liable if harm results because he does not have them. Sometimes this is called the skill of the "average" member of the profession; but this is clearly misleading, since only those in good professional standing are to be

57

considered; and of these it is not the middle but the minimum common skill which is to be looked to. (Prosser, 1971, pp. 162-163)

At first blush, it would appear that the standard is not particularly demanding, but it will emerge that this is not a safe assumption.

Writing on psychiatric malpractice, Wilkinson (1982) addresses the accuracy of judgment that is required to fulfill the standard of care: "An error in judgment is not actionable [when the clinician acted] in good faith, had made sufficient inquiry and examination into the cause and nature of the patient's disturbance, had exercised the requisite care in making the diagnosis and prescribing treatment, and otherwise had not deviated from generally accepted standards and practices" (p. 75). Leesfield (1987) states: "To establish therapist liability it must be shown that the course therapists pursued was clearly against the treatment their profession recognized as correct" (p. 57).

There is no one mental health standard of care. Elements that would seemingly be common to every mental health practitioner, such as diagnostic skill, are indefinite and inconsistently applied in legal proceedings.

Part of the difficulty in defining a standard of care comes from the fact that there are so many different types of mental health professionals: "Its diverse practitioners have completed varying educational programs and are licensed and organized into disparate groups" (Leesfield, 1987, p. 57).

Since mental health professionals are not homogeneous, public policy will allow a certain degree of individuation of the standard of care. Nonetheless, a mental health practitioner must sort through legal principles to deduce from what sources he or she can derive a standard of care. Without knowing the appropriate standard of care, preventive measures to avoid malpractice cannot be determined.

The standard of care is defined, established, and maintained by the *particular practitioner* and an *amalgamation of professional sources*. All the views and preferences are subject to the approval or disapproval of public policy, as implemented through regulatory agencies and the courts.

The practitioner influences the standard of care by what he or she purports to be offering to the public. The offering may be in the form of direct indications, such as in promotional materials, or indirectly, such as the reputation cultivated for the mental health service or the practitioner.

Mental health professionals have an affinity for credentials. In each of the mental health disciplines, a plethora of certifications is available. Some of these sources are highly reputable, like the Academy of Certified Social Workers or the American Board of Professional Psychology, and have stringent requirements for proving training and competency. However, many other sources are of dubious legitimacy.

The dubious sources may have honorable objectives and prestigious personages affiliated with the board of directors, but the unmasked intent is to garner application fees for income (often for only a few founding members of the board) and to provide a quasi-certification. It is "quasi-certification" because there is no real evaluation of training or competency performed, only a nominal qualification of holding a relevant academic degree, professing specialized training and experience, and making a payment.

The original intention for certification sources was to provide an opinion from peers to the public about who within their disciplinary ranks was viewed as qualified to provide specialized services. "Presentation of one's credentials, preparation of a work sample, and open review by one's peers are unique opportunities for the professional, which have rarely occurred to most since the defense of their dissertations in graduate school" (Baker, 1983, p. 1365). Certification was not intended to denote "the cream of the crop," only those who were qualified to practice in a particular area of service.

In the intervening years, specialized certification has taken on new meaning. Since some of the examinations were demanding, those who were successful in becoming certified tended to present their qualifications as being *exceptional* or superior to the qualifications of other practitioners in the area of service.

More recently, the plethora of specialized certification sources, which emulate the accoutrements of status (but without the academic-clinical rigor) of the legitimate certification sources, have relied on another objective: an appeal to the practitioner's vanity, by allowing him or her to use a title relevant to an area of expertise or specialization.

The foregoing discussion has two messages. First, it may well be that there is *no longer a need for any certifica-*

tion sources. Today there is a well-developed governmental regulatory system (e.g., state licensing of mental health practitioners) that more ably accomplishes the original intention that justified establishing specialized certification sources, as well as other supports for conveying information about practitioners to the public (e.g., national registers of health care providers). Second, and of relevance to this book, any certification or designation influences and potentially elevates the standard of care that will be applied to the professional's services, thereby creating more latitude for a malpractice suit.

What the practitioner holds out as qualifications to the client *and/or* what the client has a reasonable basis for believing the practitioner's qualifications to be will cast the framework for the standard of care for a malpractice case. Therefore, it may be counterproductive to display certificates from an array of specializations. If the practitioner has a credential that reflects a specialization for which he or she lacks training and competency consonant with the qualifications possessed by professionals who are, in fact, trained and competent in the specialization, he or she will have to perform services at the elevated level.

Earlier in the chapter, mention was made of the "locality" rule versus the national "specialist" rule. Local practices are still relevant for certain aspects of standard of care, and the prudent practitioner should accommodate the professional consensus in the community. Compliance with the preferences and practices of local/regional peers is useful to establishing fulfillment of a reasonable standard of care, but it goes further. When confronted with a malpractice action, the defendant-practitioner does not need his or her local counterparts testifying about his or her deviancies. To the contrary, support from local practitioners is needed. A plaintiff-client would have quite a challenge to prove malpractice if several mental health practitioners, respected in the community and known to the judge and jury, appeared on behalf of the defendant-practitioner and spoke favorably about his or her standard of care.

The standard of care requires that the professional intervention rest on a theory or school. "A 'school' must be a recognized one with definite principles, and it must be the line of thought of at least a respectable minority of the profession" (Prosser, 1971, p. 163).

The court is willing to allow a certain variety in professional preferences, but the ideas cannot be too far out of the mainstream.

> Where there are different schools of medical thought, and alternative methods of acceptable treatment, it is held that the dispute cannot be settled by the law, and the doctor is entitled to be judged according to the tenets of the school the doctor professes to follow. This does not mean, however, that any quack, charlatan or crackpot can set himself up as a "school," and so apply his individual ideas without liability. (Keeton et al., 1984, p. 187)

In a review of legal opinions on the issue of the school of treatment, Glenn (1974) concludes that an unusual or "nontraditional" psychotherapeutic approach would likely be compared to the next closest, but better established or more accepted, school of therapy.

Experience supports that the court is apt to expect every psychotherapeutic intervention to be compatible with the qualities of the psychodynamic approaches. Public policy recognizes, through judges and jurors, psychoanalytically oriented and, more recently, behavioral-modification ideas.

At this point, it seems that a reasonable standard of care will not accommodate any theory or school that is maintained with apostolic zeal. Regardless of the practitioner's preferences, every theory or school must achieve some unification with psychodynamic concepts. Even behavioral modification or behavior therapy are best brought into the fold of reasonableness by emphasizing the cognitive restructuring that occurs. Humanistic approaches sorely test the standard of care, unless presented by academic principles, research-based strategies, and purposeful treatment objectives.

The foregoing might seem to reflect a legal preference for "tradition for tradition's sake." That is not true. The court recognizes the need to encourage innovation, but not at an undue risk to the client.

> Difficulties arise when the psychiatrist wishes to pursue a new treatment, but at the same time does not want to risk exposure to potential liability should the treatment prove ineffective, or even

harmful to the patient. In such a situation, one must balance the need to protect the patient by assuring that only proven treatments are used, with the need to develop new methods that produce even better and more effective results . . . . What is clear, however, is that unless modern psychiatry is allowed to explore new methods of treatment, the future growth of the profession and discovery of new cures will be greatly inhibited. On the other hand, the patient should not be the guinea pig for every psychiatrist who has a "new, revolutionary" technique. (Wilkinson, 1982, p. 76)

The foregoing is applicable to practitioners in each of the mental health disciplines, but recall the caveat:

The willingness of some courts to indulge experimentation, however, should not be read as giving license to the reckless abandonment of knowledge and logic. Professional actions should always be predicated upon a scientific or academic rationale. (Woody, 1985a, p. 517)

Too many mental health professionals seem prone to rely on the "art" of psychotherapy after they have been in practice awhile, whereas the court always searches for the "science" of psychotherapy when deciding upon a standard of care to impose on a malpractice case.

In addition to the shaping done by the individual practitioner, the standard of care applied in a malpractice case is defined, established, and maintained by an amalgamation of professional sources. Foremost, national professional organizations influence the standard of care through dissemination of codes of ethics and specialty guidelines for delivery of services.

A position statement by a professional organization, including its code of ethics, has no legal authority *per se.* Often these statements are intended to promote the interests of the organization as an institution, although the ostensible goal is to further the interests of the membership and society.

While practitioners seem to place great importance on organizational proclamations about what should and should not be done, the courts are more reserved. A court will typically strain to give deference to professional preferences for practices, but will evaluate the ideas according to what will best serve society and uphold public policy. This caution, which is not skepticism *per se*, comes from the belief that the professions have failed in their attempts at self-regulation and have abused the public-policy trust by furthering their own interests, as opposed to the interests of the public (Bierig, 1983).

On the other hand, state statutes and case rulings have often relied on the positions maintained by professional organizations on behalf of their disciplines. For example, although unwilling to relegate regulation to the professional organizations, the state licensing law and its subsequent regulations and rules will commonly embrace the gist of disciplinary ethics and service-delivery guidelines.

When expert testimony is offered to the court, the results of research studies and opinions from recognized authorities in the field will be welcomed by the court. At all times, however, none of these voices is determinative. It is up to the trier of fact (the judge and/or jury) to weigh the applicability of the professional views about what should comprise the standard of care.

In defining a standard of care, as necessary to avoid malpractice, the practitioner must accept and comply with the positions taken on critical issues by the foremost professional organization for his or her discipline. For example, any psychologist must allow the American Psychological Association's "Ethical Principles of Psychologists" (1981a), "Specialty Guidelines for the Delivery of Services" (1981b), and "General Guidelines for Providers of Psychological Services" (1987) to govern his or her practices—even if he or she is not a dues-paying member of the American Psychological Association. Each mental health discipline has position statements comparable to these examples from psychology.

If the practitioner has an identity tied to more than one discipline or specialty, then the relevant standards from the multiple sources must be considered. For example, the psychologist, social worker, or mental health counselor maintaining a specialty in sex therapy should have training comparable to what is required for the status of Certified Sex Therapist (even though certification is not sought) by the American Association of Sex Educators, Counselors, and Therapists, and adhere to its specialized code of ethics. This principle is applicable to all dual-identity practitioners, regardless of discipline or specialty area.

The views of professional organizations will be presented to the court by other mental health practitioners who offer expert testimony about the standard of care. Often, an attorney will seek an expert with prominence on a national or international level, as a way of trying to impress the court with what should or should not be applicable to the instant malpractice case.

VICARIOUS LIABILITY

Not only must a practitioner be concerned about how well he or she fulfills the standard of care, there must be vigilance to insure that associates fulfill the standard of care. This responsibility for associates involves the *vicarious liability* principle:

> Clinicians should not only conform their own practices to appropriate standards of care but should also strive to assure similar conformity by team members, supervisees, partners, and others for whose malpractice they may be held to answer. In this regard, it is most prudent for clinicians to assume that they *will* be liable for the negligent acts of their team colleagues, supervisees, and partners. Such an assumption, while not always valid, will lead to the exercise of greater care by clinicians in their professional relationships and, therefore, to the minimization of the potential for malpractice claims. (Woody, 1985a, p. 522)

There is never any preordained framework for vicarious liability, and every practitioner should give careful consideration to this risk before accepting an affiliation with another practitioner.

The legal strategy is one of initially filing the complaint against anyone who could have feasibly prevented or contributed to the prevention of the act that resulted in the alleged injury. While money is not the answer, vicarious liability may obtain when two practitioners reap any remunerative benefit from their connection. This benefit involves more than a sharing of the profits; it could include benefiting from reducing "overhead" expense by sharing an office suite and the support operations, making mutual referrals, strengthening the reputation of the "group" practice, or receiving consultation.

The test probably comes down to whether public policy would support that the first practitioner had a duty to safeguard the clients seen by the second practitioner, and thereby should be vicariously liable for any negligence created by the second practitioner. Clearly someone designated "supervisor," including the professor who supervises a university trainee, could be held to have a duty to protect the clients of the supervisee. Likewise, when several practitioners band together to form a group practice, for whatever reason and regardless of the contract that they draw up between themselves, the clients could reasonably assume that there is a sharing of benefits and each practitioner has a duty to assure quality treatment by the other practitioners. Being "on call" for a colleague or doing a special service (e.g., a diagnostic evaluation) for the clients of a colleague would likely create vicarious liability.

Some practitioners erroneously believe that they can avoid vicarious liability by signing a document declaring that each practitioner in the group is an "independent contractor." Professionals who rent space to another practitioner often have such an agreement and unwisely believe that there is no possibility of their having vicarious liability.

To be an "independent contractor," several conditions must be fulfilled, such as (in brief) showing that the practitioner works in multiple locations and does not derive all or most of his or her income from the one affiliation. If two affiliated practitioners receive mutual benefits or do not satisfy the rigorous legal test for independent-contractor status, or if some other condition creates a duty to be responsible for safeguarding each other's clients, vicarious liability will vest, notwithstanding a contractual agreement to the contrary. There are, however, means for minimizing vicarious liability, as will be presented later in this book, and ways to agree on the financial burden associated with vicarious liability, such as an indemnification contract (see Woody, 1988).

IMMUNITY

In the earlier discussion on defenses to a malpractice action, no mention was made of immunity. The reason is simple: Immunity for professionals has seemingly met its demise and is no longer a viable defense.

In days gone by, public policy allowed a charitable institution to be exempt from liability for torts; this was known as "charitable immunity." Similarly, public policy recognized that many problems would result from imposing liability on the government, so it issued "governmental immunity."

As the years passed, public policy increased its recognition of the rights of the individual to be free from harm and to receive a remedy when damaged. The Federal Tort Claims Act in 1946 gave general consent to suing the government, but with limitations and exceptions.

Of importance to mental health professionals employed by public institutions:

> The statute retains the immunity for all governmental conduct that involves "discretionary functions or duties." The main idea here is that certain governmental activities are legislative or executive in nature and that any judicial control of those activities, in tort suits or otherwise, would disrupt the balanced separation of powers of the three branches of government. Indeed, judicial review of major executive policies for "negligence" or wrongfulness might well operate to make the judiciary the final and supreme arbiter of government, not only on a constitutional level, but on all matters on which judgment might differ. (Keeton et al., 1984, p. 1039)

This same type of governmental immunity for *discretionary functions* still applies *under some circumstances* to the planning and policy development in public mental health facilities.

Immunity does not allow the governmental agency or employee to escape the duty to warn of risks created by the discretionary functions. The provision of services, such as therapy in a public mental health facility, is known as *operational* or *ministerial functions*. The facility or the employee (including, perhaps, an administrator or board member) has no immunity from a lawsuit for injury caused by operational or ministerial functions.

There is no one test that will assuredly separate discretionary acts from operational acts—there is often overlap:

> Although the fact that the government has omitted to act is not in itself a defense, the discretionary immunity is frequently emphasized in nonfeasance cases. On the other hand, where the government's activity is affirmative, specific, and in violation of a statute, regulation or constitutional provision imposing a duty upon the government, courts are often willing to say there is no room for discretion. The presence of a pre-existing safety standard, or any appropriate standard governing the activity in question, will also tend to displace the room that otherwise exists for government discretion and immunity. (Keeton et al., 1984, pp. 1041-1042)

In other words, there is no definitive federal guideline. Essentially, each case will be interpreted, to a large extent, on its own merits.

States tend to follow the federal law, but not always. There are many different versions of immunity, and about 60% of the states have abrogated immunity in a substantial way. States may well have special procedural limitations relevant to immunity. While there is sovereign immunity for legislative and judicial decisions, those persons who implement the decisions will have less protection, such as personnel with state regulatory agencies.

Many malpractice cases have denied immunity to mental health professionals because, although employed in a governmental or charitable facility, their functions were clinical and thus not protected by discretionary immunity. The same case can potentially grant immunity to some of the parties, namely those who engaged in planning or formulating policies, and impose liability on some of the other parties, namely those who implement the planning-policy ideas in clinical services.

One view, which is by no means universal, is that if the governmental service has a commercial counterpart, there will likely be liability for torts. Suffice it to say that the health practitioner has very little to bank on in assuming that there will be any protection by immunity from legal action, especially if it is a clinical service.

CONCLUSION

The contents of the first two chapters in this book clarify the public-policy considerations and legal system for malpractice. The thrust of mental health services into the world of business has brought on many options for a cause of action against a mental health practitioner, and these continue to expand. It is incontrovertible that the number of ethical, regulatory, and legal complaints against mental health practitioners is escalating, and that malpractice is an everyday risk. The material in this chapter defines negligence and standard of care, the two primary dimensions of a malpractice action.

With the foregoing psycholegal framework, the focus will be on practical guidelines for avoiding malpractice in mental health services. Many of the principles presented in the preceding chapters will be reintroduced and elaborated upon, to accommodate preventive planning and action. Reinforcement of legal fundamentals will also be a goal for the guidelines.

Chapter 4:
The Professional-Self
Concept

The onslaught of malpractice legal actions against mental health professionals can best be countered by heeding "forewarned is forearmed" and "an ounce of prevention is worth a pound of cure." By being mindful of the legal tenets of malpractice (as described in the preceding three chapters) and tailoring one's personal qualities, professional skills, and practices to a preventive framework, the risk of a malpractice legal action can be minimized.

A preventive or proactive approach to avoiding malpractice in mental health services requires that the practitioner embrace certain principles and make adaptations in his or her personal-professional self-concept. While the essential principles of practice can usually be understood and accepted at a cognitive level, making personal adaptations requires introspection, self-evaluation, resolution of conflicting emotions, and accommodation and change at a fundamental personality level. Once the personality has begun to shift, so too must the behavioral set shift. Malpractice is, therefore, avoided by maintaining a personal self-concept, derived from personal qualities and behavior patterns that are consonant with public policy, law, disciplinary ethics and standards, and client needs.

In our contemporary society, one's occupation or career—particularly a *professional* career—carries the potential for determining an entire style and quality of life. Psychological needs are satisfied by the rewards of work. Employment affords the resources for the person and all of his or her family members to have or be denied access to certain opportunities, such as education, health services, recreation, and so on. In turn, the domestic conditions influence interpersonal relations, such as between spouses. Career and the self are fused. Thus, the threat of malpractice impinges upon the overall life of the professional, and the motivation for making adaptations in practice to be legally safe has deep-seated roots.

Conversely, the personal self-concept is related to professional practices. The professional who has personality-based doubts about his or her adequacy or competency is apt to serve clients with much less success than the practitioner who has cultivated and achieved a reasonable degree of psychological health.

Although it is beyond the scope of this discussion, there is ample documentation from psychological research for the assertion that *personal self-concept can convey power for health and achievement.* In day-to-day professional operations, the "power of the self" is fueled by an ever-present awareness, at both the conscious and unconscious levels, that proper and adequate service is attained through a complementarity of personal needs and professional objectives.

The guidelines for avoiding malpractice that are presented in this chapter are predicated on the necessity of accommodating career-related considerations in one's personal set. Achieving an "examined self" and having a reasonable compatibility with the demands of the profession are prerequisites for entry, and are of no less importance than having the academically based skills and the terminal degree required for gaining employment.

BEING WHAT YOU ARE PREPARED TO BE

A major source for legal complaints is a professional's ill-conceived, overzealous, or untrue representation of qualifications. While sometimes a manifestation of pathology or dishonesty, in most instances the *faux pas* comes from being foolishly caught up in pursuing career, monetary, or egotistical gains.

*GUIDELINE 1: DO NOT ACCEPT A POSITION
FOR WHICH YOU ARE NOT FULLY QUALIFIED*

It is well and good to aspire to career advances. Unfortunately, this legitimate quest is sometimes contaminated, such as by an employer who recognizes that an illustrious job title or assignment with authority (over others) can be used to save financial resources.

Public policy has been an unwitting accomplice to abuse of titles. Many states do not require licensing of psychologists when they are employed by a nonprofit health care facility. Needing employment, one man, with a legitimate doctoral degree in a nonmental health field, was flattered by and accepted an offer to be a "psychologist" for a large hospital that decided that saving money for salaries was preferable to having a well-trained, but higher-paid, staff. The pseudopsychologist was assigned difficult clinical cases, did not receive close supervision, and was soon sued for malpractice.

Another scenario commonly encountered in mental health services involves either the newly graduated or the displaced professional. When a preferred form of employment is unavailable, unwise judgment—exercised for survival—leads to accepting a job for which the individual has inadequate personal or professional preparation. While an EdD degree in student personnel services, an MSW degree in *macro* social work, or a PhD degree in experimental psychology are *bona fide* credentials, the majors stated are not clinical in nature. I have encountered several situations where professionals have, by economic necessity or egotism, accepted clinical positions and then had ethical, regulatory, or legal actions brought against them.

Numerous professionals, faced with a legal action, have acknowledged that they were "swimming in deep water," but they did not know how, or lacked the personal fortitude, or felt helpless to get out of the high-risk situation. This age of cutbacks in funding for mental health and the plethora of university graduates trained in mental health services has led some professionals to become private practitioners prematurely. They must then function without the knowledge or clinical acumen adequate for meeting the standard of care required for the clientele, and without colleagues readily available to provide supportive consultation and backup services.

GUIDELINE 2: DO NOT USE VANITY CREDENTIALS

Mental health professionals can look in magazines and newsletters and find advertisements for becoming "Diplomated" or "Certified" in some exotic specialty. To be sure, there are respectable and valuable credentials that can carry a title, like Diplomate (such as awarded by the American Board of Professional Psychology), or convey certification (such as awarded by the Academy of Certified Social Workers). Some other sources, however, do little more than gratify a vain need and can be gained by payment of a fee with minimal, if any, documentation of professional qualities.

The respectable and valuable credentials are usually gained only by examination (rarely by a "grandparent" clause), and require a work-sample evaluation by a panel of recognized specialists. If a credential is awarded merely by having a qualifying degree (such as holding a doctorate or master's degree) *and* paying a fee, it should be suspect.

A credential of dubious legitimacy will increase the risk of a malpractice action. Any credential used *in any way* for professional posturing carries connotations for what the clientele can reasonably expect from the practitioner, and thus has implications for the standard of care that would be applied in a malpractice legal action. But it goes further.

While a court will typically *strain to uphold the professional* in a malpractice legal action, it will do so only if the professional can document that the omissions or commissions with the client, upon which the malpractice action is based, were reasoned, well-intended, and respectful of the client's rights, dignity, and welfare. If there is a smudge on the honor of the practitioner, he or she will likely encounter a reversion by the court to, perhaps, use the situation to teach the entire profession a lesson (recall the discussion on punitive damages in Chapter 3).

Besides bestowing a title like Diplomate or certifying competency in a practice specialty, there are sources for obtaining a doctorate degree without going through the rigors of a university or professional-school training program. Often these doctorates are advertised as "the degree you deserve" and indicate that there will be an evaluation of "the applicant's life experiences" to partially fulfill the requirements for the degree. Of course, another factor that will partially fulfill the requirements for the degree is a hefty payment.

Some of these sources state they are "licensed by the state." Such licensure usually has no relevance to quality or accreditation of training—rather it means that the source has paid for a business license to operate.

To be legitimate, a degree must be from a program that is regionally accredited by an accreditation source recognized by the U.S. Department of Education. Further, it is possible to have a properly accredited degree (even from a major university), that still does not conform to the academic requirement that a state board of examiners might require for licensing—which has definite relevance to the standard of care that would be applicable in a malpractice action. For example, to be eligible for licensure as a psychologist in the state of Florida, the applicant must have a doctorate from a training program that is accredited by (or equivalent to) the American Psychological Association. There are many university training programs that would not meet (or be equivalent to) those accreditation standards.

The underlying legal principle for avoiding malpractice is a version of the "clean hands" doctrine, which holds that gaining unfettered judicial support requires an impeccable status. To register a helpful defense and benefit to the fullest from it, the professional should be free from any wrongdoing. Even a semblance of dishonor, or being self-serving at the expense of or risk to the client, could lead to a less than optimal view from the judge or jury.

PROFESSIONAL DEVELOPMENT

Critical protection from allegations of malpractice can be obtained from professional affiliations. Public policy has accepted professionalism as an important dimension of societal organization, and is willing to allow—to a limited degree—self-determination by members of a profession. It should, however, be added that the escalation of professional liability (as per Chapter 1) is partly due to a failure of professional self-regulation (e.g., ethics committees). Public policy has been altered to impose accountability through governmental regulation (e.g., state licensing boards) and the legal system (e.g., malpractice actions). Nonetheless, malpractice can be avoided by alignment with professional standards.

GUIDELINE 3: AFFILIATE WITH STANDARDS-SETTING PROFESSIONAL ASSOCIATIONS

Joining professional associations satisfies many purposes. A professional association can promote disciplinary

73

interests (such as championing legislation or promoting positive public relations), provide information and training (such as publishing a scholarly journal), and cultivate a sense of professional identity for the membership (such as by appreciating what others in one's discipline are doing and advocating).

Becoming a member of a professional association does not, in and of itself, provide a legal safeguard against malpractice. But if the association sets standards for practice, and the professional adheres thereto, such disciplinary definition for practice would surely receive worthwhile consideration and, to a reasonable degree, deference by the judicial system.

Obviously, it is *not enough just to affiliate* with any association. Indeed, there may be inadequate reason to become a dues-paying member *per se.* The important issue is that standards for practice promulgated by a professional association gain credence from public policy. The practitioner who can assert and document allegiance to such standards will be wrapped in the protective cloak of professionalism.

GUIDELINE 4: CLAIM NO SPECIAL EXPERTISE OUTSIDE OF NATIONAL STANDARDS

As explained in Chapter 3, the standard of care that will be applied in a malpractice action will consider how the reasonable and prudent practitioner in a like situation would have performed. Historically, the comparison was with a professional of the same degree, training, and presumed competency in the immediate locale. This "locality" rule was based on the belief that standards might differ due to barriers to the practitioner's staying abreast with research and advances in the discipline, and the uniqueness of each community. The availability of professional journals and continuing-education opportunities, as well as the mass media, air travel, and the influence of national professional associations, have led to a decrease in reliance on what is done or not done by practitioners in the immediate geographical area. Rather, it is now recognized (with a few exceptions) that a standard of care may well be defined at the national level. But it goes further.

In malpractice actions, when a practitioner holds himself or herself out as, or the client has a reasonable basis for believing that the practitioner is, a "specialist" in a particular area of mental health service, a national standard will be more likely to be accepted than if there has been a message to the consumer that he or she is a "general practitioner" of the mental health discipline. Some states recognize this national "specialist" standard of care by statutory law.

Being a "specialist" is likely to impose a national, as opposed to local, standard of care, *and* elevate the competency that will presumably be aligned with the reasonable and prudent practitioner in that specialty of mental health care.

Many mental health practitioners believe that declaring themselves specialists will facilitate successful competition in the marketplace. It is reasoned that there is prestige associated with being a specialist, as opposed to being a general practitioner. Consequently, an advertisement (such as in the yellow pages of the telephone directory) may contain a list of specialty services. Such a listing may backfire. One client said, "I saw Dr. X's ad, and I knew immediately that no practitioner could do all of those things equally well." Also, the listing likely imposes a higher (specialty) standard of care than would be applied to a listing of general practice.

Sometimes the professional does not assert specialization directly, but allows (consciously or unconsciously) certain messages to be conveyed to the client that support an impression or belief that he or she has special expertise. For example, one professional attended a 3-day training program on behavioral medicine at a prestigious university, and then included "trained in behavioral medicine at XYZ University" in his brochure. Placing certificates of attendance in short courses or membership in associations on the waiting-room wall, or leaving numerous pieces of reading material on a particular topic on the waiting-room table, can foster a reasonable belief in the mind of the client that the practitioner has the competency of a specialist.

Since the legal test will consider whether or not the client's belief was *reasonable*, regardless of what the practitioner did or did not directly assert, it is imperative that caution be exercised to avoid misimpressions. Messages to clients should be assessed for what is *implicit*, as well as what is *explicit*.

In the event that there is a legal action and the elevated "specialist" standard of care is applicable, the practitioner's actual competence may matter little. Instead, the standard for competence will be derived from, for example, what is advocated by legitimate specialty certification sources. Therefore, the relevant standards to be satisfied by a practitioner who professes to be: a marriage and family therapist might come from the American Association for Marriage and Family Therapy; a sex therapist might come from the American Association for Sex Educators, Counselors, and Therapists; clinical hypnosis might come from the American Society of Clinical Hypnosis; and so on—regardless of whether the practitioner is or is not affiliated with the relevant organization. Note that the foregoing associations are cited as examples, and do not necessarily constitute the *only* associations that might set standards, including those for the specialties mentioned.

If the practitioner holds a special certification, such as being a Diplomate from the American Board of Professional Psychology, the standard of care would likely be dictated by others who hold the same national credential. It would not be dictated by professionals in a more generic sample, such as the membership of a division of the American Psychological Association. This same principle applies to the other mental health disciplines.

PERSONAL MONITORING

Regardless of training or experience, every practitioner is, at some time, vulnerable because of personal difficulties or professional shortcomings. Clearly, the legally safe approach is to develop means to: (a) monitor for problems and prevent their occurrence; and (b) capitalize on virtues and skills.

GUIDELINE 5: AVOID
AN ISOLATED PRACTICE

People differ in their needs for independence or dependence, and mental health professionals are no exception. Being totally independent can create an unhealthy isolation from the mainstream of professional thought. More problematic, unilateral decision making and judgment can be faulty. Lacking in the detached, hopefully more objective views of a colleague or supervisor, the isolated practitioner faces great risk from making an omission or commission in client care.

Isolation is potentially troublesome for all types of professionals, but it is especially difficult for the mental health professional. The intense and highly personal nature of, say, psychotherapy imposes peerless pressure on the therapist-client alliance. The vicissitudes of everyday life can lead the professional with the best of training to sometimes make judgments or behave in a manner that is not truly in the best interest of the client.

Personal problems that are exacerbated by isolation and the emotional press of clinical practice foster a special vulnerability, allowing the therapist-client relationship to move to an unacceptable status. A later guideline will explain the importance of serving strictly as a professional to the client.

As will be discussed in more detail shortly, supervision from a colleague provides an important monitor for the standard of care and, should there be an allegation of malpractice, a source for verification of commitment to client welfare. Short of supervision, the same principle obtains: Having a colleague with whom ideas and therapist-client conflicts (such as countertransference responses) can be discussed will help in keeping the client's treatment regime within the scope of the acceptable standard of care.

GUIDELINE 6: MAINTAIN A SUPERVISORY RELATIONSHIP

In accord with the foregoing guideline to avoid an isolated practice, it is important—no, imperative—that every mental health practitioner maintain a communication channel to another professional who can offer consultation and supervision. This is true for every practitioner, regardless of advanced training or seniority in the field. And it is an ever-continuing necessity.

From a legal point of view, malpractice is avoided by having a source to verify (or testify) that the practitioner was: (a) desirous of meeting the client's needs and welfare; (b) open to having a critique made of the service (there was nothing surreptitious to hide in the treatment or the therapist-client relationship); and (c) conscientious about meeting an acceptable standard of care. If a practitioner has openly presented a case to a supervisor, received suggestions, and attempted interventions accordingly—yet negative results occurred with the client—it would be very difficult for an allegation of malpractice to survive in the judicial system. A professional does not have to be perfect, only to adhere to an acceptable standard of care.

The form of supervision can vary according to the relevant conditions. For example, the psychological condition of one client might be so tenuous or severe that extensive supervision would be necessary, whereas supervision might be almost nominal for another, less troubled, client. Likewise, a professional might have greater expertise with one treatment strategy and need little in the way of supervision, yet have lesser expertise with another treatment strategy that would call for more thorough supervision.

The need for supervision varies at different points in the practitioner's personal sphere. Virtually every professional suffers from human frailties on some occasions (say, at the time of a divorce or "midlife crisis"), and will then need closer supervision than at other times. When these conditions occur, it behooves colleagues/supervisors to step forward and forcefully move the practitioner toward a client-centered set.

The preferred approach would be to have supervision from an objective "outside" professional, one with no conflict of interest. On the other hand, pragmatics may dictate that an associate in the same practice be used as a "sounding board" and that supervision be less formal (more will be said in Chapter 5 about colleagues being aware of each others' cases to avoid malpractice and vicarious liability). Any supervision is better than no supervision.

In accord with a later guideline about conceptualizing one's career in a long-term perspective, today's public policy recognizes mental health services as constituting a business. From the private practitioner's entrepreneurial efforts to the charitable facility's competing for tax, grant, or United Way dollars, the goal is to establish a financial base. As with any business, this means investing (prudently, of course) in necessities to further the operations. In this litigious era, one of the best investments that can be made is to purchase supervisory time from a highly trained professional. To try to "bootleg" or "freeload" supervision is to allow a miserly view to prevail over reason and logic.

GUIDELINE 7: SEEK CONTINUING EDUCATION

Just as one never outgrows the need for supervision, there should be an ongoing commitment to seek continuing education. A mainstay of professional negligence has long been *currency*, as would allow the practitioner to complement client care by embracing ideas and techniques derived from new or recent research. Consequently, public policy has shaped legislation (in some states) to require a certain number of approved continuing-education units (CEUs) per year to maintain a license to practice. It seems likely that this license-renewal requirement will become more widespread in the future.

Regardless of a license-renewal requirement, professional ethics routinely endorse principles on behalf of client welfare that make it necessary to keep up-to-date with research and professional ideas. While an ethical principle will not necessarily determine a malpractice question, the court's deference to the professional will likely be stronger if he or she has ethical underpinnings, such as having sought to provide "progressive client care," with a continuing-education record to document it. In straining to uphold the professional, the court can be expected to want to see an indication of commitment to excellence in client care. A useful index is the professional's ongoing (and hopefully systematic) effort to enhance his or her competency, such as through continuing education.

BEING A BUSINESS

To have optimal protection against legal complaints, mental health services should be tailored for business effectiveness. This means: (a) having a clear *statement of purpose* and *service perimeter* (a guideline in Chapter 6 will deal with the importance of having a restricted scope of service); and (b) maintaining a personal allegiance to the human-service *business* enterprise.

GUIDELINE 8: CONCEPTUALIZE YOUR SERVICES AS A BUSINESS

As elaborated upon in Chapter 2, society has come to believe that *mental health services are part of the health care industry*. Clients are mindful of the monetary requirement, and they consider the mental health practitioner to have a rightful expectation of a payment for services (although some clients try to deny their financial responsibility by reverting to an "I deserve charity" or "I am entitled" posture).

Despite the clear-cut societal support for the mental health industry (e.g., encouraging third-party payments) and its willingness to accept entrepreneurial efforts by mental health practitioners (e.g., accommodating advertising of and professional service corporation benefits for mental health services), the practitioner may still be inclined to conceptualize his or her practice as a humanistic endeavor. Of course, any mental health service does and should have a distinct humanistic component, but the *contemporary* framework for mental health service is as a business entity.

If the practitioner fails to base planning and decision making on the commercial or business foundation, the service structure will be faulty and the possibility of inept handling of liability-related matters will be present. The practitioner who retains a realistic commitment to human service, *and* manifests that commitment via a service-delivery model that is compatible with the existing socio-economic dicta for business operations, will be on much firmer ground if or when he or she is subjected to an allegation of malpractice.

For the practitioner with training rooted several years in the past, it may be difficult to recognize that: (a) the ethical parameters for practices that were inculcated in the formative professional years no longer fully obtain; and (b) today there is a powerful business orientation for client care. There seems to be a reluctance to relinquish early-acquired ideas, yet those once-useful ideas can now jeopardize making legally safe judgments.

For example, there was a time when a client would not sue a therapist. In part, this was due to the stigma attached to having others know that the client was receiving mental health treatment. Now there is far less concern about "going public." Since mental health professionals have become part of the health care team, as witnessed by their being employed in physical-health facilities, there is little distinction made by a litigious client about filing a legal complaint against a physical versus a mental health care giver.

One remnant of the past that is particularly troubling is the therapist's belief that "no matter what arises, my

client and I should talk it through." While such a con-
frontation is ostensibly for the potential therapeutic
growth of the client, today this notion also masks the
therapist's denial of the nature of litigation. Various
psycholegalists have commented that a mental health professional is often his or her own worst witness in the face
of a legal complaint (more will be said about this matter
in a later guideline on being appropriately defensive
when a complaint arises).

It must be remembered that when a client files a
complaint: (a) anything said by the clinician is subject to
selective and distorted interpretation; and (b) the therapeutic alliance is no longer sacrosanct—the dyad has been
augmented to be a triad. The client's attorney now influences the client's thinking and screens the professional's
comments for what could lead to an admission of wrongdoing or breach of the standard of care.

GUIDELINE 9: KEEP YOUR CAREER
IN A LONG-TERM PERSPECTIVE

Given that today's mental health service is a business,
the practitioner must respond to day-to-day events like a
business person. Mental health professionals are steeped
in emotional struggles, presumably on behalf of the
client's welfare. When a complaint about one's clinical
practice arises, it carries the potential of cutting to the
core of the professional's identity and, in the process,
provoking a response that, while understandable because
of human nature, would lead to deleterious effects for the
business. The business framework requires that plans,
decisions, actions, and reactions be calculated to enhance
the long-range development of the commercial operations.

With elevated emotions—as might be provoked by an
attack on one's career—the practitioner is more vulnerable, as opposed to responding rationally and logically. It
is common for a therapist to instruct a client who is experiencing a crisis that "these things too shall pass" and to
offer guidance in rational-emotive strategies. Often, the
same therapist will experience extreme stress and faulty
reasoning when a complaint occurs. Certainly, the therapist would do well to "practice what you preach."

A complaint commonly creates so much disruption for
the practitioner that he or she becomes obsessed with the
matter, suffers negative emotional and behavioral consequences, and wants, above all else, a quick resolution to

the conflict. It is well-documented that: (a) the legal system seldom allows a quick resolution for any conflict; and (b) an effort to gain a quick resolution will likely lead to a higher price being paid (in emotions, reputation, or money) than allowing the legal process to follow its natural course. As difficult as it may seem, sometimes allowing time to pass actually serves to benefit the practitioner (e.g., the client-plaintiff may not have suffered as extreme, if any, injury as was initially alleged). The old adage "haste makes waste" has relevance.

GUIDELINE 10: FOLLOW A
CAREER-INVESTMENT STRATEGY

In a broader sense, a legal safeguard results from keeping a career in long-term perspective. The professional who tries to promote his or her practice at a rapid rate may be prone to not think through the alternatives adequately and thus make poor judgments.

In terms of advancing the mental health business, there will rarely be a situation that demands immediate action. More often than not, the passage of time for analysis, reflection, and careful decision making will not lessen the immediate profits or benefits. Instead, careful calculations will circumvent conditions that might be fertile for a legal complaint. "Fools rush in where angels fear to tread" offers a worthy philosophy for long-range business operations.

The wise practitioner should be far more interested in what will be accomplished over several decades of work than what can be obtained quickly and easily. As opposed to "high-risk, quick-gain" investments, one's career should be tailored to be a "low-risk, sure-gain" investment. Given the time, money, and ego that are invested in obtaining training and licensure, this axiom is incontrovertible for the professional.

GUIDELINE 11: INVEST IN ALLIES

In this day and age, every successful business has underpinning from expertise other than the principal's. Most commonly, a business person's essential allies are an attorney and an accountant. For example, the world of state and federal taxes alone constitutes a course that cannot be wisely charted without legal and accounting navigation. Perhaps of equal importance, every decision maker can benefit from objective counsel, such as having another professional with whom ideas and options for the business operations can be discussed.

Notwithstanding their advanced training, mental health professionals are often reluctant to turn to an outside consultant for ideas about conducting a clinical practice. Perhaps this reluctance stems from the highly personal nature of mental health services. It may be reasoned, "unless you're a therapist yourself, it is impossible to sense all the considerations of deciding on how to practice."

The reluctance to seek needed allies may also come from naïveté about how to conduct a business. Precious few, if any, mental health training programs offer even a modicum of exposure to business methods. When discussing this lack of training, one professor commented: "If they want courses on business, they can take them after they get in practice—my job is to train them to be good clinicians." In this litigious era, I would submit that the "cart before the horse" must be guarded against. I would ask: "How can one be a *good* clinician without knowing how to practice in accord with societal requirements and with finely honed business skills?"

There may be a third reason for not relying adequately on allies: frugality. Contrary to the sometimes-heard stereotypes about "wild-eyed therapists," mental health professionals, as a group, are rather conservative—particularly about money. This likely comes from the fact that their incomes were, in the past (more so than today), relatively meager, and they were often employed as "public servants" (such as in community mental health facilities).

Frugality can be a virtue, but in today's business arena and given the ominous presence of malpractice, frugality can lead to unnecessary vulnerability to complaint. From my experience with mental health professionals, many legal actions against them could have been avoided by having received and heeded legal or accounting advice.

Some practitioners commit hours of time to doing their own bookkeeping, when a fraction of that amount of time spent at income-generating work would have paid for a bookkeeper and allowed leftover time for healthy pursuits (like recreation with family members). When this sort of expenditure of valuable time occurs, there is reason to question the practitioner's personal-professional wisdom. There are many business-related activities that should be performed by others, if for no other reason than to allow the practitioner to pursue a healthy mind and body, thereby allowing the practice to be optimally performed.

Many practitioners are reluctant to pay for consultation, even though they do not hesitate (quite correctly) to charge for their consultation to clients. Attempts to "get free legal advice" from an attorney-friend or to get tidbits about taxation in casual conversations with an accountant brings to mind the adage: "You get what you pay for!"

The wise business person knows that commercial success depends of investing in support services. As the mental health professional enters the business world, it is necessary to adopt a receptive attitude for *prudent and essential investments.* One such investment is to obtain expertise from professional allies. Having an attorney and an accountant readily accessible will offer much-needed protection from allegations of malpractice. More will be said in Chapter 6 about proper reliance on legal counsel.

GUIDELINE 12: CARRY MALPRACTICE
INSURANCE AND UNDERSTAND THE POLICY LIMITS

The security afforded by insurance scarcely needs mentioning. With the ever-present specter of malpractice looming over the mental health service, the practitioner should arrange for adequate malpractice insurance coverage. Unfortunately, "adequate" coverage may be difficult to achieve.

The major national mental health associations offer malpractice insurance policies to their members. Presumably because of the large number of members, the "group policy" is easily affordable. Even if the policy costs several hundred dollars, it may well be worth it. Conversely, it is also possible that an insurance policy could cost very little and not be worth it.

An insurance policy specifies the limits of coverage. Thus, it may exclude certain acts, such as any sexual misconduct by the professional. It may have special conditions; for example, one group policy reportedly covers only those cases where the practitioner is upheld.

Perhaps of greater concern, some policies may contain wording that is nebulous and poorly defined. This ambiguity leaves the practitioner with a lack of specificity for what is or is not covered by the insurance. An unclear or a nonspecific definition of coverage could lead to a dispute between the insurance carrier and the practitioner as to whether a particular alleged omission or commission was within the coverage of the policy. If there is a legal complaint, one of the last things needed by the practitioner is a lack of clarity and/or a controversy with what was believed to be his or her protectorate—the insurance company. If that unfortunate scenario should occur, it could mean the added problem of the practitioner's suing his or her own insurance carrier, thereby seeking a court order for insurance coverage of the malpractice action.

In conducting seminars, I routinely ask how many of the mental health professionals in attendance carry malpractice insurance. Usually most indicate that they do (or they believe that they are covered by their employer's malpractice insurance, which will be discussed further in Chapter 5). When these insured practitioners are asked how many have read the policy, it is rare to have more than a very few raise their hands (usually fewer than 5%).

Of those who have supposedly read the policy, few can answer simple questions about it, such as "Can you select your own attorney?" and "What if the insurance company wants to settle the case and you do not want to do so?" It would be the rare (if not nonexistent) group insurance policy, as available through a national mental health association, that would provide as broad and as detailed a coverage as would ideally suit the practitioner, or allow the insured-practitioner to retain unilateral determination of the selection of an attorney or the decision to accept or reject a settlement opportunity.

The alternative to a low-cost group policy would be to have an insurance policy tailor-made to the practitioner and the features of his or her practice and clientele. Aside from the cost that would likely attach to such extensive coverage, few, if any, insurance carriers are open to such idiosyncratic policies in this era of escalating professional liability.

As will emerge throughout this book, the best protection from a malpractice complaint is a carefully planned and executed professional practice. While insurance does not afford all-encompassing protection, it is an important adjunct to a careful professional practice set. When a policy is obtained, however, it must be studied and understood, and its tenets must be accommodated in clinical decision making and practices.

Chapter 5:
The Company That
You Keep

There is much to be said for and against having associates. On the positive side, the nature of mental health practice can be emotionally draining and lonely. Having colleagues in the practice can provide emotional support. This offers a safeguard against the development of an ethically and/or legally inappropriate condition between the client and the professional (such as might accommodate sexual misconduct).

Having another practitioner readily available yields professional benefits. Ideas can be shared for enhanced client care, and there will be an opportunity for professional stimulation. A colleague can also offer case consultation or supervision, as would assist in contradicting an allegation of breach of an acceptable standard of care.

A group practice affords distinct financial benefits. Referrals can be exchanged "in-house," which minimizes the possibility that a client will gain primary attachment to another set of practitioners. The overhead expenses (e.g., rent, secretarial service, etc.) can be shared. If the practice is successful enough, there may be financial benefits (such as for tax purposes) from becoming a business entity, such as a partnership, a corporation for profit, or a professional service corporation (see Woody, 1988, for more details on becoming a business entity).

But there is also a down-side to having associates. Stated simply, any connection to another practitioner creates the potential of incurring vicarious liability for his or her conduct (see Chapter 3).

Vicarious liability is predicated on the notion that since professional associates benefit from their affiliation and each is in a critical position to safeguard the clients—fulfilling the public-policy dictate for welfare and safety in exchange for professional status—legal liability will attach to all professionals concerned with the enterprise. This potential for vicarious liability will obtain regardless of who had the primary contact with a client.

It should be pointed out that the standard of care for the practice of law necessitates the attorney's naming every potentially liable person as a party to a malpractice action. Moreover, in championing the best interest of his or her client, the attorney wants to maximize the chances of gaining a remedy. Thus, while one mental health practitioner might be primarily responsible for a negligent act, if he or she has no assets and there is a second practitioner who has assets for remedying the damage to the client, the second practitioner might well end up paying more than the primary wrongdoer. Stated differently, the attorney wants to reach the "deep pocket," the source of the most assets.

In suing associates, the attorney fulfills the standard of care for the practice of law by naming all who have a reasonable degree of possible liability. As more is learned about the conditions surrounding the alleged malpractice (i.e., as the case matures), it is possible for previously named defendants to be dismissed from the action.

GUIDELINE 13: KNOW YOUR COLLEAGUES

Vicarious liability can attach for the conduct of a layperson employed by the professional. That is, the principle of *Respondeat Superior* holds that the professional (the "Master") is potentially responsible for damage created by the employee (the "Servant"). If the omission or commission occurred within the employee's scope of duty, the employer is likely to be liable for the damages. It is feasible that the employer could seek redress from the employee for, say, negligence, but the action would nonetheless name the employer.

To avoid malpractice emanating from an employee's conduct, the employing professional must carefully select every employee for suitability for client care. An employee should not be selected solely for technical skills. Thereafter, the professional/employer must maintain a training and monitoring program to assure that the employee does not create any undue risk for a client or the professional. If the professional is to counter *Respondeat Superior* liability, it will be necessary, among other things, to prove that every reasonable step had been taken to safeguard clients from employee misconduct and that the employee's allegedly wrongful conduct was outside the scope of duty and was performed by the employee "while on a personal frolic."

This same sort of precautionary stance must be maintained with professional colleagues. Too often, it seems, professionals affiliate with each other for the wrong reasons. One of the most frequent reasons is to cut down on overhead expenses. The vicarious liability that attaches often far outweighs the relatively small amount of money that is saved on shared operating expenses.

Some associations are formed by people who just happen to come together, such as having been graduate students in the same classes or employed in the same agency. Any association should be based on the members' fulfilling the prerequisites of adequate professional training and competency, personal compatibility, shared goals, and reciprocal benefits (such as providing complementarity).

Before the association is cemented, there should be total personal and professional revelations. Whether or not there is a business entity with a statutory requirement of a fiduciary duty, each associate should be compelled to work for the best interests of the other associates.

Full disclosure encompasses both personal and professional factors. Despite the crucial nature of disclosure and the legal authority for fiduciary duty, mental health professionals are prone to neglect an adequate development of mutual understanding.

On a personal level, if there is maladaptive behavior (such as substance abuse or risky sexual preferences), it should be acknowledged, even if it jeopardizes the likelihood of formulating the association. Likewise, a joint undertaking, including a clinical association, should consider each person's financial picture. It bodes ill for an association if, say, one professional is a fiscal conservative (e.g., does not buy anything on credit) and the other professional spends liberally. It is also suspect if one would-be associate has much more in savings and assets than the other would-be associate. Joint and several liability could lead to a disproportionately large financial obligation on the professional with assets, notwithstanding an equal or greater degree of wrongdoing by an associate with fewer assets.

On a professional level, there should be a thorough understanding by all concerned of theoretical and technical priorities, and a willingness to make related adjustments to safeguard each other. Certainly every associate should restrict his or her services to areas for which he or she has clear academic documentation of preparation—yet it is the rare practitioner who voluntarily produces a transcript of university coursework. In a clinical association, prudent practitioners should require such a disclosure, and be willing to exchange any and all information that has relevance to client care and professional *and* personal reputation.

Although it is beyond the scope of this discussion, every professional association should be structured to attain maximum legal protection. In brief, a business entity can accommodate statutory requirements, business efficiency, debtor liability, and investment and tax benefits, but it can seldom do more than minimize the possibility of malpractice (such as, depending on the laws unique to the state, the use of a professional service corporation). While a corporation may be used to shield personal assets from corporate debts (such as for leases and purchases), it does not eliminate the possibility of a malpractice action directed at both corporate and personal assets. (The relevant statutes of each state are different, and specific legal counsel on this matter is advised.)

GUIDELINE 14: PROVIDE SUPERVISION

In the preceding chapter, gaining personal supervision was endorsed as a means to minimizing and countering an allegation of malpractice. Supervision is also important to protect against vicarious liability.

Extrication from a suit alleging vicarious liability will be furthered by proof of having exercised reasonable (or greater) care through supervision. No matter how well-trained or experienced, every practitioner can gain legal protection from receiving supervision. Any association of practitioners should have a continuing arrangement for supervision. While this supervision could be legitimately gained from each other, it is most protective to obtain the *objective* services of an "outside" professional, thereby contradicting any inference of a conflict of interest.

Trainees create a special problem. Many practitioners sense a chance to give something back to the profession by, or gain a satisfaction from, having graduate students affiliated for a practicum or internship experience. This is a worthwhile undertaking, but it can be fraught with liability. It is common for the "field supervisor" (i.e., the practitioner) to have little or no say about who is assigned to him or her and no in-depth knowledge about the trainee's personal qualities and professional competencies.

When a trainee first enters a practicum or internship, the supervisor is likely to make a greater effort to monitor the trainee's services than as the training wears on. Good intentions, especially (it seems) in private-practice situations, seem to wither under the press of pragmatic conditions, such as generating income or meeting a heavy client demand for service.

To avoid malpractice, the clinician-supervisor should exercise no less (and possibly more) caution in screening and selecting trainees than in employing support personnel or accepting a professional associate. Once a trainee has been accepted, there should be a plan maintained for case assignments, treatment decisions, and other supervisory matters. If time does not allow for close supervision, the practitioner should not succumb to the enticement of accepting a trainee.

GUIDELINE 15: FILE WRITTEN OBJECTIONS

Often a facility will accept trainees (or beginning clinicians) and assign them to a senior clinician, who will be told by a superior administrator: "We have a training mission and the trainee will be assigned to you, but we cannot afford your spending much time actually supervising." When this occurs, the supervising clinician must recognize that, regardless of the administrative order, he or she may potentially incur personal liability for the conduct of the trainee.

Frequently it is asked: "If I file an objection to the administration, won't I be able to avoid vicarious liability?" The answer, unfortunately, is "not necessarily." The answer would apply to many other situations where the clinician objects, perhaps in writing and repeatedly, to an administrative policy or order, but continues on the job—there could still be liability. Incidentally, the difficult thing to accept in these situations is that the administrator who functions only in a policy role might be able to invoke immunity which would be unavailable to a clinician carrying out orders.

This same sort of situation can develop between peers in the same clinical practice. For example, one professional may believe that a partner in practice is not maintaining an adequate standard of care or is on a hazardous personal track that will jeopardize the safety and welfare of clients. Filing a written objection is helpful, but does not guarantee that there will not be liability, such as for the wrongdoing of the peer.

Whether an employer-administrator or a peer-colleague, public policy supports that objections should be made to rectify the situation for the best interest of the client and society. In the event the rectification is not attained, the clinician may have no alternative but to create a barrier to liability, by disengaging from the employment or clinical association.

GUIDELINE 16: REQUIRE A DETAILED JOB DESCRIPTION FROM YOUR EMPLOYER

For the mental health professional employed by another practitioner or by a health care organization, it is best to have a detailed job description. The first guideline given for avoiding malpractice (see Chapter 4) involved not accepting a position for which you are not qualified. There is no way to evaluate suitability for a position without knowing categorically and with precise detail what duties are assigned, what service is to be performed, and what supportive resources are available.

Some employers prefer to say: "Let's just work out the details of your job assignment as we move along; I'm sure we can agree on it later." While appealing, such an evolution can play into possible liability for malpractice. Circumstances could lead to a task assignment for reasons other than competency, and the risk of a complaint would be elevated.

A job description offers important employment and legal security for both the employer and the employee. First, both parties solidify their mutual contractual commitments by a meeting of the minds about what will be the consideration provided by each of them. Second, the employer will know what services can be competently staffed by the new employee. Third, the employee will have a perimeter of responsibility, along with a delineation of resources for quality control (e.g., available consultation, supervision, referral sources for particular cases, etc.). Fourth, any unattended risks can be detected and eliminated. If there is a pitfall, the employer can obtain other resources to remedy the situation, and the employee, by a protective wall of defined duties, can stay distanced from the concomitant liability.

GUIDELINE 17: HAVE A CONTRACT THAT SPECIFIES YOUR EMPLOYER'S LEGAL LIABILITY

Informal surveys in my seminars support that the employed professional commonly believes that he or she will be covered against any malpractice action by his or her employer's professional-liability insurance policy. Such may or may not be the case.

Typically I ask: "How many of you who believe that you have malpractice coverage from your employer have actually read your employer's policy?" There is almost never anyone who has seen a copy of the policy. When asked, "Why not?" the answer is often: "They won't show it to me." When asked, "How do you know that you are covered?" the answer is usually something like: "Well, my boss said I was covered." To the obvious follow-up question, "Covered for what," the universal answer is "I have no idea."

A lot of professional-liability insurance policies cover any damages incurred by the employer because of the employee's conduct, but they do not cover the *personal damages* assigned to the employee. In other words, if the attorney filed a malpractice action, named a therapist personally and the employing clinic, as *Respondeat Superior*, and received a judgment against them, the insurance policy might cover the portion of the judgment (which could be all, partial, or none of the damages) assigned to the employer. With this example, the amount assigned to the employee personally would have to come from a separate insurance policy (as the clinician might purchase through membership in a national professional association) or personal assets.

Seldom will an employer's personal-liability insurance policy provide funding for the employee to select and pay for an attorney to represent exclusively his or her legal interests. Instead, the professional will either have to use personal funds to hire an attorney, or rely on the attorney who has been retained to *primarily serve the employer or insurance carrier*, and who may end up trying to assign all the liability to the employee by a cross-claim.

Any employer who will not provide an employee with the details of an insurance policy that allegedly covers malpractice should be suspect. If there is nothing to hide, there should be no concern about disclosure of the terms of the policy. Keeping all concerned persons, management and employee alike, fully informed will create legal safeguards for both the employer and the employee.

In the event that an employer does not provide malpractice insurance, either for all employees or by providing the funds for the employee to purchase it elsewhere, the employee should consider having an indemnification clause in the employment contract. The employer can agree, by contract, to indemnify the employee for any legal expenses, attorney's fees, judgments, and so on, incurred by the employee as a result of working in that employment setting. Of course, some employers will not agree to such a clause or will want a reciprocal agreement from the employee (i.e., that he or she will indemnify the employer), and the financial liability and risk may be so extreme that it is illogical to be employed therein.

An indemnification clause is only as strong as the wording of the contract *and* the assets of the indemnification source. There are clinical facilities that appear, by brick and mortar, to be substantial operations, but their financial status is so tenuous that their assets (particularly if a corporation) may be limited, and a large malpractice judgment could surpass the assets needed to indemnify an employee.

Chapter 6:
Framing a
Clinical Practice

Avoiding malpractice can be furthered by the manner in which a clinical practice is formulated, structured, and presented to the public and other professionals. The underlying premise is that a practice geared to accommodation of public policy and professionalism will be assured, until proven otherwise, a degree of deference from public policy and the legal system. When locked in a legal battle, even a modicum of deference can produce a beneficial effect.

GUIDELINE 18: KNOW YOUR DISCIPLINARY ETHICS

Part of the escalation of malpractice can be attributed to our society's disillusionment with the efficacy of self-regulation by professions. At one time, the public and, consequently, the legal system were quite content to allow professionals to review their members' performances, and if a member should fall below the disciplinary standard, to invoke sanctions. This governance was usually implemented by an ethics committee within a professional association.

No matter how rigorously an ethics committee pursues its task, there are inherent limitations to effectiveness. An ethics committee can only respond to complaints, and if the constituency does not trust the outcome—believing "birds of a feather flock together" or "there's no honor among thieves"—the threshold to regulation will never be effectively crossed. Indeed, to a large extent, the foregoing was the public's reaction to the application and en-

forcement of ethics to mental health professionals. After
a period of trust, our society concluded that regulation by
ethics was insufficient for the task.

Even after a complaint has been processed, a professional association can do little except appeal to the unethical practitioner's sense of decency, which clearly is
probably not a strong point of his or her character (or
else the bad judgment would not have occurred in the
first place). At the utmost, the unethical practitioner, usually after repeated violations, can only be "drummed from
the corps," and this may be a rather small price to pay for
someone who was not motivated to conform to disciplinary standards.

With some practitioners, there may be no ethical
source with "jurisdiction." If a wrongdoing practitioner is
not a member of any relevant association, there is no ethical committee to which a damaged client can turn.

All of these limitations added up to the public-policy
support for governmental regulation, such as through a
state licensing board. Through state licensing, society has
a vehicle to move the errant clinician into a criminal
courtroom, to a closely supervised (probationary) continua-
tion of practice, or out of the profession in that state
altogether. Of course, there may be an unlicensed practitioner who can escape the licensing arm of governmental
regulation—in those instances, the doors to the courtroom
are open to the wronged client.

Although it could be asserted that professional ethics
have been diminished in importance, at least for finding
redress for injured clients, they are still alive and well
for the practitioner who wishes to find means for avoiding malpractice. While not legally determinative, professional ethics are viewed by the court as a source by which
alleged malpractice can be scrutinized. The prudent practitioner should steadfastly maintain allegiance to an appropriate ethical code, thereby gaining protection from a
malpractice complaint.

*GUIDELINE 19: KNOW YOUR DISCIPLINE'S
GUIDELINES FOR DELIVERY OF SERVICES*

Closely akin to relying on professional ethics to shape
a legal appraisal, the court's willingness to uphold a
practitioner will be furthered by setting forth evidence of
how: (a) the standard of care was derived from guide-

lines promulgated by the relevant professional discipline; and (b) all services to the client were consonant therewith. As with ethics, service-delivery guidelines will not necessarily be determinative of a legal question, but they certainly hold the potential to be influential.

Unfortunately, specific guidelines for the delivery of services are not well developed for all mental health disciplines. Perhaps the prototype is the American Psychological Association's "General Guidelines for Providers of Psychological Services" (1987) and "Specialty Guidelines for the Delivery of Services" (1981b), which offer important (but voluntary) standards for the clinical, counseling, industrial/organizational, and school psychology specialties. Other national organizations for mental health professionals are known to be moving in the same direction, and it is predicted that such specialty guidelines will become more and more available and influential in establishing the standard of care for legal actions.

GUIDELINE 20: KNOW LEGAL
PRESCRIPTIONS AND PROSCRIPTIONS

While professional ethics and specialty guidelines carry only the potential to shape legal thought about an alleged breach of a standard of care, state statutory law possesses unequivocal legal authority. The preponderance of legislative law relevant to malpractice is at the state level, but certain federal acts, such as the Education for All Handicapped Children Act, the Rehabilitation Act, and the Family Educational Rights and Privacy Act, may contain provisions that relate to standard of care.

Of special importance, a state statute to license the practice of a particular mental health profession will commonly set what should or should not occur in the practice of the profession. If there is an alleged violation of the codified standards, the client filing the complaint may go first to the state department of professional regulation (the name will vary with the state government) for a disciplinary measure, or directly to a court of law for a judgment—or both the state department and the court can be petitioned.

In addition to legislation, the state courts will produce a myriad of opinions in case or "common" law that will define standards for professional conduct. The difficult thing about case law is that not all opinions are published, there may be contradictory opinions in the same state, and the opinion may be distinguished in such a way as to make instant application tenuous at best.

Being well-informed about the law governing a state is no less important than being well-informed about professional ethics and special guidelines for the delivery of service. Indeed, many legalists argue that being knowledgeable about the law is far more important than disciplinary ideas. Regardless, many professional training programs provide only scant coverage of ethical matters and almost no preparation in the legal aspects of professional practice.

Avoiding malpractice will be strengthened by a conscientious and consistent adherence to the legal directions afforded by statutory and case law. If the practitioner has not received formal training in the legal aspects of his or her discipline, a remedial effort should be initiated (e.g., systematic reading, continuing education, consultation from an attorney, and so on).

GUIDELINE 21: KNOW PUBLIC POLICY AND COMMUNITY STANDARDS

Notwithstanding their authority, legislative and case laws are always subject to interpretation. While all-encompassing legal principles may be the first consideration, the deliberations by judge or jury will inevitably be idiosyncratic to some degree. For example, even if a national standard of care is appropriate for a malpractice case, the nature of the trier-of-fact (i.e., the judge or jury) will lead to consideration of how like professionals in the community conduct their practices and what the local citizens expect for an outcome. Public policy has many layers. There can be a national health care policy, which is implemented by state legislative actions (e.g., appropriations) and is prioritized, accepted or rejected, and sanctioned by qualities and preferences unique to the locale.

Malpractice must be declared by a "jury of peers," and public policy and community standards will be weighed heavily in the determination. While not determinative legally, these special idiosyncratic and parochial foci will clarify the application of more general legal principles to the case at hand.

GUIDELINE 22: CULTIVATE COMMUNITY AND PROFESSIONAL SUPPORT

After the public policy and community standards are understood, it becomes necessary to tailor practices to accommodate them. Fundamentally, it is a matter of conducting one's clinical services in a manner that "wins friends and influences people." Lest this sound too self-serving, conducting a clinical practice along this line will, of course, benefit the practitioner, but it will also benefit the clientele by serving as a motivator for the practitioner to live up to the expected standard of care.

In terms of avoiding malpractice, community and professional support will create a barrier to an unjust lawsuit. If others in the community have reason to believe that the practitioner is conscientious about a client's welfare and impeccable in maintaining safeguards and quality, it will be difficult, at best, to get another professional in the community to give expert testimony (which is almost always necessary in a malpractice case, even if "outside experts" are brought in to testify about the national standard of care) to establish a breach of the standard of care. The testimony would more likely turn out to be a learned explanation of how, if there were injury to a client, it was unforeseeable and/or unavoidable, and that the defendant-practitioner had functioned at an acceptable level of professionalism.

GUIDELINE 23: PRESENT YOUR PRACTICE MODESTLY

Related to cultivating community and professional sources, it is apparent that a surefire way of producing negative attitudes from laypersons and professionals alike is to adopt a flamboyant style in clinical practices. While it can be argued that the accoutrements of success (e.g., an expensive home and automobile) can foster an impression that will enhance the business, there is also the risk that such "baubles and bangles" will be interpreted by some people as being in poor taste and ostentatious.

Advertising a professional service is both legal and ethical, as long as it is honest and not misleading. While Supreme Court rulings require circumscription, certain guidelines for advertising may be adopted for a profession. In fact, the business nature of mental health services indicate that an effective advertising plan should be implemented. However, it has been repeatedly evidenced that professional colleagues are readily alienated by an advertising campaign with which they can find fault. In selecting an approach to advertising, some concern should be given to how other professionals—even if they are competitors—will react to the advertisements.

Provoking a negative reaction, especially from professional counterparts who believe there will be a fallout to their status and image, can create enemies. When a lawsuit for malpractice is threatened, one of the last things needed is a coterie of local professionals ready to testify, "The defendant never did act like a good clinician."

The foregoing is a bit of oversimplification, but it is intended to convey that modesty is sometimes a powerful preventive measure. This leads to endorsement of the technique espoused by Gerald Caplan, MD. When offering ideas about how to be an effective mental health consultant, Caplan (1970) recommended that the consultant (who was commonly more expert than the consultee) emphasize how he or she was less capable than the consultee. He termed this paradoxical strategy "one-downmanship."

In promoting a clinical practice, the temptation is to try to outshine the competition, such as by generating fame. Such a strategy may serve primarily to motivate the competition and lead them to search for flaws. Therefore, when a complaint is lodged, they are ready to speak against the defendant-practitioner. Fame then gets transformed into infamy. Malpractice can be avoided by one-downmanship. Turning competitor-colleagues into allies makes them feel that they are important to your success—which is true.

GUIDELINE 24: SELECT AN APPROPRIATE FORM OF BUSINESS

As mentioned earlier, becoming a business entity, such as by incorporation, does not necessarily provide any immunity from a malpractice action. Selecting an appropriate form of business for a clinical practice can, however, minimize the possibility of a legal action as a result of an erroneous structural issue.

It is beyond the format of this book to explain the various alternative forms for a clinical business. Details on and guidelines for selecting a form of business are available in Woody (1988). Herein, the focus will be how the form of business can help the clinician avoid malpractice.

The four basic forms for a business are: the sole proprietorship, the general partnership, the limited partnership, and the corporation. With each form, there will be state statutes that provide legal definition. Each state has its unique legal conditions. It should be emphasized that all of the comments in this section are generic, and the statutes of a given state may be different. (See "A Cautionary Note" in the front matter of this book.)

The *sole proprietorship* is sort of a nonentity. The sole proprietor stands alone in the marketplace. Other than accommodating tax deductions for necessary business expenses, there is little about the sole proprietorship that provides protection from a malpractice complaint.

In theory, a *general partnership* can exist with or without a formal agreement. A debt incurred in the name of the partnership carries personal liability for each partner. If the debt exceeds the partnership assets and the *pro rata* share of each partner, the excess can attach to the assets of any partner with additional assets. Vicarious liability is exacerbated by the principle of joint and several liability. As Olle and Macaulay (1986) state:

> All partners are jointly and severally liable for the partnership's tort and breach of trust liabilities and are jointly liable for all other civil liabilities. When liability is joint and several, an action for the full amount of the liability may be brought against one or more of the partners. When liability is merely joint, all partners must be served in the enforcement action if they are within the jurisdiction of the court and are not bankrupt. (p. 73)

The partnership carries considerable liability. Given the reciprocal benefits derived from the association, there will likely be an inherent duty to supervise and safeguard all clients seen by any of the partners, and a partner is likely be liable for the malpractice of another partner.

A *limited partner* is simply an investor. While sharing the profits and losses, it is feasible that a limited partnership would allow for certain limited partners to be shielded for malpractice liability—but only if they could establish that they had no duty to monitor, supervise, and correct the clinical practice of the general partners.

A *corporation for profit* can be useful in a mental health practice, such as for restricting debts to the assets of the corporation (no personal liability for the shareholders). This shield, however, is not raised for malpractice. That is, should a corporate shareholder be a clinician and have a malpractice complaint filed against him or her, the action might reach the corporation's assets, the defendant's personal assets, and (especially if there were a duty to supervise and/or vicarious liability could be established) the other shareholder-clinicians' personal assets.

Some states have offered a bit of relief from vicarious liability by a statute for a *professional corporation.* Much like the corporation for profit, a professional corporation allows an association of shareholder-practitioners from the same discipline (states vary on the latter restriction) to reap the benefits of corporate business and tax law. A single practitioner may also rely on a professional corporation; that is, multiple shareholders may not be necessary. Overcast and Sales (1981) provide information on psychological and multidisciplinary corporations.

Relevant to avoiding malpractice, the professional corporation may afford limited protection from vicarious liability. The Florida Statute states:

Nothing contained in this act shall be interpreted to abolish, repeal, modify, restrict, or limit the law now in effect in this state applicable to the professional relationship and liabilities between the person furnishing the professional services and the person receiving such professional service and to the standards for professional conduct; provided, however, that any officer, agent, or employee of a corporation organized under this act shall be personally liable and accountable only for negligent or wrongful acts or misconduct committed by him, or by any person under his direct supervision and control, while rendering professional services on behalf of the corporation to the person for whom such professional services were being rendered; and provided further that the personal liability of shareholders of a corporation organized under this act in their capacity as shareholders of such corporation, shall be no greater in any aspect than that of a shareholder-employee of a corporation organized under [the corporation for profit act]. (Florida Statutes, 621.07, Volume 3, 1985, pp. 390-391)

The delineation of liability within the foregoing statute does not construct an impermeable barrier. An enterprising attorney would seek to establish that the other shareholder-professional(s) had the errant "person under his direct supervision and control" and, even with the afforded corporate protection, it might be necessary to defend against vicarious liability.

Selecting a form of business can foster an incentive for improving operations. As an intelligent person, the mental health professional may draw from the business form an incentive for studying the manner in which clinical practice is conducted and implementing new and improved methods. This quest for improvement, tied to maximizing the business to its ideal form, will provide an element of protection against conditions that might breed a cause of action for a malpractice complaint.

GUIDELINE 25: OPERATE ACCORDING TO A RISK-MANAGEMENT SYSTEM

Having a risk-management system involves far more than simply being cautious. Another book (Woody, 1988) covers risk management in the broad sense. It points out that, by definition, risk management encompasses being adequately insured, making wise investments, defining an appropriate scope for mental health practice, establishing a standard of care that fulfills legal requirements, having policies with legal safeguards, selecting a useful form of business, using prudently planned marketing and advertising methods, managing employees or human resources and client accounts wisely, and maintaining effective operations.

Many of these risk-management components underlie the guidelines set forth in this context for avoiding malpractice. Risk management yields benefits well beyond avoiding malpractice *per se*, but as a concept, it is certainly central to negating any condition that could lead to an allegation of malpractice.

It is not the purpose of this book to teach risk management; that sort of information is available elsewhere (Woody, 1988). Rather, the emphasis at this point is on the necessity of having a risk-management system within which all clinical services are conducted.

Adopting a few isolated risk-management techniques will, at best, have a shotgun effect. Choosing a few risk-management techniques will most likely lead to alleviating the risk associated with the more glaring problem areas. Malpractice seldom occurs from only one flaw (unless it is powerful enough to infect the entire system).

Avoiding malpractice is best obtained by systemic protection. This requires: (a) understanding the composition (e.g., the purpose, resources, etc.) of the clinical practice; (b) selecting strategies for goal attainment (along with analytic and evaluative safeguards); and (c) identifying the forces that will impinge, positively and negatively, on the systemic effort.

The prudent mental health practitioner should maintain a system for recognizing and accommodating the inter-relationships of the myriad of risk-related factors endemic to clinical services. The practitioner who plunges ahead without a systematic approach is precariously tempting malpractice. Operating by a risk-management system will offer reasonable assurance that no seeds of client discontent will blossom into a malpractice complaint.

Chapter 7:
Client Management

In its most basic form, an allegation of malpractice is an attestation of ineffective client management. If the practitioner is sensitive to client needs and offers services according to an acceptable standard of care, it is improbable that a client, regardless of his or her mental condition or the treatment outcome, will come forward with a complaint. Therefore, the practitioner facing an allegation of malpractice should recognize that, by the mere occurrence of the complaint, he or she did not properly execute client management.

REGISTERING INTO A CLINICAL PRACTICE

Legal safeguards can be obtained from the time that a client first receives services from the professional. By making certain entry conditions clear to the client, there will be an implicit acceptance. With the entry conditions serving as part of the standard of care, the client's implicit or explicit acceptance supports the notion of informed consent.

GUIDELINE 26: FORMULATE A
RESTRICTIVE SCOPE OF SERVICE

Heretofore, several guidelines expressed the notion that the practitioner should not accept a job assignment or take on duties for which he or she has inadequate personal and professional preparation. Similarly, the practitioner must guard against the temptation of having an expansive scope of service, as might lead to inept involvement in certain kinds of client problems.

Some practitioners seem to believe that the more skills or the greater competency that they profess, the more they will hone their competitive edge. The opposite may also be true. If they over-reach, they will, sooner or later, be "cut down to size," such as by an allegation of malpractice.

An acceptable standard of care requires that the practitioner consistently manifest at least the minimal level of required competency. While it is desirable to cultivate new professional knowledge and skills, this must be done in a calculated, professionally accepted way. Self-ordained competency is unacceptable; there must be professional documentation, such as through formal training or supervised experience.

Earlier, I cautioned against proclaiming special expertise, unless there is certainty of meeting national standards. Whether a specialist or a generalist, the practitioner having an expansive scope of service must demonstrate competency up to the standard of care relevant to *every* problem area or form of intervention that is offered to clientele.

If the clinician is a general practitioner, the scope of service will be broad. The term "general practice" provides no justification for a diminution of quality care. In fact, being a general practitioner puts the onus of achieving extensive competency—and intensively maintaining it—directly on the clinician. Liability will attach if the quality of service falls short of the standard of care for each problem or intervention. The distinction between the specialist and the generalist is that the specialist will likely have a substantially higher standard to meet than the generalist, but the latter is not excused from meeting a general-level standard.

Avoiding malpractice is furthered by having a scope of service that is restricted to areas or strategies with which the practitioner is personally comfortable and professionally competent. A realistic assessment of strengths and weaknesses should be interfaced with what is necessary to compete successfully in the marketplace. If this produces dissonance, it is premature to enter practice, and adaptations (such as gaining additional training or seeking a different practice context) must be made.

GUIDELINE 27: KNOW YOUR STANDARD OF CARE AND COMMUNICATE IT

After settling on a scope of service that is protected by assured competency, the scope of service should be translated into a written standard of care (as per the tenets set forth in Chapter 3 and relevant guidelines herein). The standard of care is not a guarantee, but it will be viewed legally as an admission of intention for quality.

Some practitioners "puff" their services. That is, they center their promotional message on self-aggrandizement. This is ill-advised.

In marketing a product, public policy supports claiming superiority to the competition, but a distinction is made for professional services. While a salesperson can get away with heaping praise on a product and exalting the "buy of a lifetime," the public looks askance at a professional's claiming superiority or exuberantly proclaiming the need for his or her services.

The possibility of malpractice is increased whenever the professional professes exceptionality over the prevailing standard of care. Not only may the standard be elevated, there may be a negative psychological reaction from clients, the community, and professionals, which would increase the likelihood of a litigious or oppositional motive.

A standard of care, couched in professional language and geared to the reading ability and comprehension of the layperson, should be promulgated to all who will consider it. It is useful to have a brochure that states the restrictive scope of service, the standard of care, and policies (such as arrangements for payment). This kind of informational document should be available to every client (and his or her immediate family members) from the first contact with the mental health practice.

Having an established business routine of providing a standard-of-care document means that the client who pursues treatment with the practitioner is deemed to have implicitly accepted the standard of care (assuming that the client is mentally competent). The principle of "informed consent," a prized public-policy condition for acceptable health care, will have been at least partially attained.

To promote informed consent, the practitioner must: (a) provide the client with continual information about interventions, such as about side effects, limitations, alternatives, and probable degree of efficacy; and (b) gain voluntary, informed, and knowledgeable acceptance by the client throughout the course of treatment.

GUIDELINE 28: ENTER A SERVICE CONTRACT WITH CLIENTS, WITH NO GUARANTEED OUTCOME

The notion of a service contract with client should not be confused with a behavioral contract, wherein the client agrees to follow certain behavioral prescriptions to further therapy. Rather, a service contract documents what services the practitioner has agreed to provide to the client, *and* the conditions for therapist-client relationship.

The service contract benefits the client by spelling out what is *and* what is not to be provided, thereby stimulating client motivation for improvement. It also benefits the client by letting him or her know how the policies of the practice will be applied; the practitioner similarly benefits.

Survey data support that a large portion of malpractice complaints come from clients who owe money to their clinicians. Thus, the service document should spell out the financial arrangements, and should provide for a reasonable termination of treatment should the client fail to fulfill his or her obligations to the practitioner. More will be said about termination, referral, and follow-up later in this chapter.

While the service contract will be helpful for defining the practitioner's duties to the client and the client's rights and obligations to the professional, care should be exercised to avoid any semblance of a guarantee of treatment outcome. It is wise to include specific disclaimers of guaranteed outcomes, as well as statements about what will or will not be acceptable in the therapist-client alliance. For example, a statement should proscribe socialization between the therapist and client, and the legal requirement of reporting danger of bodily injury to self or others should be set forth to avoid any faulty idea about confidentiality.

GUIDELINE 29: SPECIFY THE LIMITS OF CONFI-DENTIALITY AND PRIVILEGED COMMUNICATION

Should the professional wrongfully breach confidentiality and/or privileged communication, the client could have several possible causes of action that would be, broadly defined, aligned with malpractice. These would include breach of contract, invasion of privacy, intentional infliction of mental distress, and others.

When there is a reasonable expectation and right to confidentiality and/or a statutory creation of privileged communication (which is almost always the case with clients who receive services from mental health professionals), the client can explicitly waive his or her protected rights by a signed release of information (more will be said on this matter later). As long as the waiver is executed with knowledge, free from duress, and voluntarily, the practitioner is on firm legal ground. A possible malpractice problem arises when the professional must release information for a public-policy reason that is against the wishes of the client and that would, under other circumstances, receive protection.

Whether by the scope-of-service document or the service contract, the client should be informed of the limits of confidentiality and privileged communication. The laws of each state will be unique on the fine points of what matters require negation of confidentiality and privileged communication.

A common reason for a question about confidentiality arises when the client is a party to a legal action, such as a divorce and child-custody dispute or personal injury litigation, and the "other side" wants to discover information about his or her mental condition. Initially, discovery is achieved through issuing a subpoena and/or taking the deposition of the practitioner. One discovery method is to issue a subpoena for a professional to produce information, be it copies of client records or professional opinions during a deposition. When a subpoena is issued, the prudent practitioner should attempt to obtain the client's express (written) approval to respond to the subpoena. If the client balks, it might be best to have an attorney file a motion to quash the subpoena, which means that the matter will be put to a judge for a ruling on whether or not the information should be provided. When the practitioner is responding to an order of the court, there will be an important degree of protection from the client's later pursuing a complaint against the professional based on alleged wrongful breach of confidentiality or privileged communication.

Perhaps more troubling, states have mandatory reporting laws. Again, the laws of each state are unique, and the practitioner should obtain legal information for his or her location. Among other things, the mental health professional may have a duty to come forward whenever there is knowledge of child abuse or danger of bodily injury to self or others—even if the client does not want the information exposed to authorities.

By informing the client from the onset of the treatment that there are limits to confidentiality and privileged communication, the practitioner will be attaining protection from a later allegation of a wrongful breach. Even so, this sort of mandatory reporting may be the trigger for the client to seek other reasons for a malpractice complaint. There is no panacea; this risk is one that goes with the times, and the only consolation is knowing that the court will strain to uphold the practitioner who has performed with honorable intent and according to the law.

GUIDELINE 30: HAVE THE CLIENT PRE-REVIEW ALL COMMUNICATIONS

Problems can arise when the practitioner transmits a communication that, while well-intended, meets with the client's disapproval. Even if the client signs a request for information to be sent (such as to another health care provider), the contents of the message must still pass the approval of the client. If the wrong thing is said or if the wording is offensive to the client, a complaint may result.

Submitting health-insurance forms for third-party payments can be risky. Since an insurance form will include a diagnosis and someone (say, an employer) might have access to that information and take a negative action against the client (an employee), it is best to have the client know and understand all information on the information form before it is sent. Ideally, the client should actually mail the insurance form, thereby providing proof that the client knew, approved of, and was responsible for the release of information. The policy could be that, even if the client signed the form and provided a stamped envelope to the practitioner, the material would be routinely returned to the client for mailing to the insurance company.

If the client does not approve of a particular point of information (say, the diagnosis), counseling about the matter should be provided. If the client is intractable, the practitioner should certainly not use less correct information (say, an unjustified diagnosis) simply to pacify the client. Rather, the client's defensiveness should be encountered, and if the defensiveness is too great for effective treatment, the possibility of termination and referral should be explored.

A similar strategy should be used with reports, such as might be sent to a physician or attorney. Even with the written consent of the client, no report should be sent without the client having seen and endorsed it.

When releasing information by request, it is best to release only information created by the practitioner. That is, even though the practitioner may possess reports received from other health care providers, the client should submit a request to the other health care providers to send additional copies to the intended source. Since a health care provider has a "limited property right" to the records and information created, each provider should control, with the client's approval, the dissemination of copies.

GUIDELINE 31: HAVE A
STANDARDIZED RECORDING SYSTEM

The client's record is probably the foremost source of information in a malpractice case. As one plaintiff's attorney said, "When I am approached by a client about a possible malpractice case, the first thing that I do is inspect the record and find out if the practitioner made a diagnosis and had a logical treatment plan." Since the entries in the record are made contemporaneously (e.g., at the time of each treatment session), the legal system tends to credit the contents of the record with honesty.

Despite the obvious legal benefits in having a standardized recording system, more often than not it seems that mental health professionals are unaware of the protection that is possible. Instead, they tend to make entries that will remind them of where they left off at the end of the last session, and they begrudgingly make hurried, scribbled comments—commonly omitting critically important details for documenting the standard of care.

A well-developed record can preclude a malpractice allegation ever becoming a complaint to the court. Before getting involved in a malpractice action, the potential attorney for the plaintiff will want to review the record. No sensible attorney will get involved with a case that does not have indicia of malpractice within the record, or for which the record at least does not contradict malpractice. If for no other reason, the attorney will avoid involvement because of the possibility of not getting remuneration for his or her efforts.

GUIDELINE 32: RECORD YOUR RESPONSES
IN AS MUCH DETAIL AS CLIENT RESPONSES

Analysis of many records reveals a failure to record what the professional communicates to or does with the client. Rather, perhaps because of the wish to use the record of a reminder of what went on in earlier sessions (to create the impression of remembering and caring about the client?), the record is generally replete with client responses.

Avoiding malpractice is accomplished by documentation of the professional's omissions and commissions. It matters relatively little what the client stated or did. What matters is how the practitioner responded and behaved in relation to the needs of the client and the individualized treatment plan.

Certainly client responses should be recorded. Beyond legal protection for the practitioner, the record must serve the client's interest in having information that can be transmitted to other health care providers, as might assist them in their services to the client. By necessity, this means providing details about the clinician's attempted interventions, the client's responses to the various strategies, diagnostic impressions, and recommendations (including prognoses).

GUIDELINE 33: KEEP AN ACCURATE LOG
OF THE SERVICES AND THEIR PURPOSES

Part of the record should include a log of every interaction with the client, and the reason that it occurred. Of special concern, unscheduled telephone calls (such as returning a client's telephone call from home in the evening) should be dutifully logged and the contents and purpose noted. Even if there is no charge for the contact, it should appear in the client's file and on his or her statement of account.

Numerous complaints have centered on the professional's allegedly having communicated or been with a client at a time or place that is not reflected in the record. If a contemporaneous note had been made about such an irregular contact, or there was a well-entrenched recording system that would have included reference to such an alleged contact had it actually occurred, the professional would most likely be exonerated.

Since money is often at issue when a malpractice complaint is formulated, there should be meticulous recording of services. An itemized account (with length of time, even if there is only a per-session charge) should be made available to the client on a regular basis. Computerized billing programs expedite this protective measure.

GUIDELINE 34: HAVE A SAFE RECORD STORAGE AND AN EFFECTIVE RETRIEVAL SYSTEM

While property law supports that the client record is the property of the practitioner, the client has a right to expect that the information will be preserved for a reasonable period of time. There is no fixed length of time for preserving the record, but ethical principles and specialty guidelines for the delivery of service often address this issue. For example, the specialty guidelines for counseling psychology state:

> The policy on record retention and disposition conforms to state statutes or federal guidelines where such are applicable. In the absence of such regulations, the policy is (a) that the full record be maintained intact for at least 4 years after the completion of planned services or after the date of last contact with the user, whichever is later; (b) that if a full record is not retained, a summary of the record be maintained for an additional 3 years; and (c) that the record may be disposed of no sooner than 7 years after the completion of planned services or after the date of last contact, whichever is later. (American Psychological Association, 1981b, p. 658)

Unfortunately, other disciplines and specialties, including some within psychology, may have different or no specified terms. For example, the document previously cited provides the following for clinical psychology:

> The policy of record retention and disposition conforms to federal or state statutes or administrative

113

regulations where such are applicable. In the absence of such regulations, the policy is (a) that the full record be retained intact for 3 years after the completion of planned services or after the date of last contact with the user, whichever is later; (b) that a full record or summary of the record be maintained for an additional 12 years; and (c) that the record may be disposed of no sooner than 15 years after the completion of planned services or after the date of the last contact, whichever is later. These temporal guides are consistent with procedures currently in use by federal record centers. (American Psychological Association, 1981b, p. 646)

Thus, if the record were not available for the time frame prescribed for the discipline or specialty, the client might rely on the specialty guideline to establish a cause of action for malpractice.

The foregoing discussion centers on avoiding malpractice by meeting the rights of the client. Maintaining an effective record storage and retrieval system also provides legal protection for the practitioner. The availability of the record can establish that the practitioner met the standard of care. Records could be needed for legal defense purposes well beyond the terms stated in specialty guidelines. Analysis of health care malpractice cases supports that records should, in all likelihood, be retained forever (Roach, Chernoff, & Esley, 1985).

Storage of records requires security. From the infamous Watergate-era break-in of a psychiatrist's office in search of a social activist's file, to a psychopathic quest to learn intimate details about a person, the files of a mental health professional are vulnerable to unauthorized invasion. While there is no known legal mandate for locks or fireproofing or whatever, logic supports that some care should be exercised to make sure that client records are secure.

Retrieval of records is often left to serendipity or luck. Many practitioners simply put old client records into boxes when their file cabinets are stuffed, place the poorly marked boxes into basements and attics, and hope unconsciously that they will never have to crawl into a dimly lit storage area and sort through the boxes in search of a specific bit of client information. The weakness in this approach and the paramount legal protection obtained by client records makes further comment unnecessary.

PROFESSIONAL POSTURE

The possibility of an allegation of malpractice will be lessened by an academically based approach to practice. Legal safety comes from an acceptable intervention theory, no illogical innovation or experimentation, a client's informed consent and reasonable assumption of risk, and clinical practices that ward off any semblance of breach of the standard of care.

GUIDELINE 35: BASE ALL INTERVENTIONS ON A WELL-ESTABLISHED THEORY

The status of being a professional rests upon a scholarly basis. In the early years, our society had reservations about the legitimacy of mental health services. There was doubt that "head shrinkers" were scientists. After having proven their merits, mental health professionals have been granted an esteemed position in our social order—but only if they fulfill the expectation of possessing special training.

The standard of care requires that the practitioner follow a school of thought that is supported by a substantial portion of the professional community. Although not stated by law *per se*, there is reason to believe that the legal system has a conservative view of psychological theory. Any untraditional approach to treatment would likely be tested against traditional approaches, to wit: psychodynamic principles (Glenn, 1974).

If faced with a malpractice complaint, it is ill-advised to present a "true believer" stance. A zealot is seldom appreciated, and certainly not in legal proceedings. Rather, being able to explain a treatment strategy by time-honored and well-accepted scholarly principles provides the practitioner with a valuable means for counteracting an allegation of malpractice. Supportive testimony by highly respected professional colleagues, who adhere to the same theoretical principles and speak favorably of the professional school of thought, buttresses the defense.

GUIDELINE 36: HAVE INNOVATIVE TECHNIQUES REVIEWED BY OTHERS

The foregoing endorsement of explaining interventions by traditional principles does not mean that legitimate innovation is frowned upon by the legal system. To the contrary, the legal system will try to support innovative procedures, but only if they have been formulated by academic reasoning, subjected to peer review within the profession, and implemented in a manner that provides reasonable safeguards to the client (with, of course, informed consent).

If experimentation is undertaken, it should be clearly labeled as such, and conducted with protective measures for the client. In granting informed consent, the client should acknowledge the experimental status of the intervention. There may be risks associated with unproven strategies that would shock the conscience of the court even if the client's consent were obtained. Public policy might negate a client's waiver of liability for a professional when the client is unable to comprehend or appreciate the severe harm that could occur.

No matter how much acceptance is expressed by a client, a professional is obligated to restrict experimentation or innovation to a reasonable degree of risk, as judged (presumably) by peer review within the profession. A profession is not free to be absolutely self-determining on these matters. If the collective judgment proved to be unwise, self-serving, or devastating in results, public policy could impose legal sanctions against the entire profession.

Just as supervision provides legal safeguards in day-to-day clinical operations, peer review puts a "stamp of approval" on innovation or experimentation. As mentioned, professional endorsement will not be an absolute ruling, but it will likely be looked on favorably by the court until proven wrong or unconscionable.

GUIDELINE 37: INFORM CLIENTS OF RESERVATIONS ABOUT EFFECTIVENESS

It is essential that the practitioner be impeccably honest. Any hint that the practitioner was less than straightforward about the effects of a treatment could lead to negativism in a malpractice case. As explicitly or implicitly included in professional-ethics codes, the client has a right to know about shortcomings of a treatment procedure. For example, a psychologist is obligated to tell a client about the fallibilities of a standardized test.

To avoid malpractice, a client should receive full disclosure about every treatment strategy. It could be argued that the client's knowing the limitations of a method could lessen the clinical persuasion that facilitates psychotherapeutic interventions and would, therefore, be to the client's disadvantage. If true, then that is one of the tolls extracted by today's litigious society.

The practitioner has a duty to the client, as well as a duty to himself or herself, that can only be fulfilled by providing the client with information about treatment efficacy. If the client does not receive this information, there is apt to be a dilution of informed consent and assumption of risk, as would support an allegation of malpractice.

GUIDELINE 38: ESTABLISH A DIAGNOSTIC SYSTEM

Approaches to treatment that bypass diagnostic methods are following a hazardous route. Although not mainline thought for all treatment theories, the prevailing legal view is that treatment should be predicated upon diagnostic impressions, as formulated by (particularly) standardized and objective procedures.

Regardless of the mental health discipline or context for practice, malpractice can be circumvented by maintaining an appraisal program. Some pundits might brand this "unnecessary protective practices that increase costs to the client." Such a view is naïve to the realities of malpractice.

Both the client and the practitioner will benefit from a diagnostic system. The client will be assured that the practitioner will have a thought-out, individualized approach to treatment—a quality that might otherwise be missing due to the hectic pace at which some clinicians are pressed to proceed. The clinician will have a scientific/scholarly basis upon which he or she tailored the treatment plan for the client, thereby gaining assurance that the standard of care will contradict an allegation of malpractice.

GUIDELINE 39: DETECT AND
REPORT SIGNS OF DANGEROUSNESS

Connected to the need for a diagnostic system, the duty to warn and (in some instances) to protect makes it imperative that the clinician initially and continually evaluate a client's potential and propensities for dangerousness or violence to self or others. Any reasonable assessment method might suffice, whether it be simple questions in an interview format (such as about suicide ideation or hallucinations involving commands to be violent) or use of formal psychological tests (such as a standardized questionnaire relevant to suicide, anger-hostility, or emotional stability). There is research to support that certain test profiles, such as with the Minnesota Multiphasic Personality Inventory (MMPI), can be used to predict dangerousness; unfortunately, the research results are sometimes contradictory (Walters, 1980).

Courts have rapidly adopted the view that a mental health professional must assess dangerousness and predict violence to self or others, even though the research supports a high degree of error or "false positives"—predicting that a client will be violent when he or she later proves not to be (Monahan, 1983). J. D. Woody and R. H. Woody (1988) provide a review of the important legal cases and public-policy issues germane to the duty to warn and protect, and offer suggestions for meeting this responsibility.

To avoid malpractice, the professional should: (a) have an established method for assessing dangerousness and predicting violence (as spurious as it may be from the vantage point of behavioral science); (b) know to whom to turn when a warning must be issued (which will vary with the client and the conditions of the case, but most often will involve family members and/or law enforcement personnel); and (c) be prepared to intervene to protect the client from his or her own violent propensity (as well as to protect the intended victim).

GUIDELINE 40: HAVE ARRANGEMENTS
FOR EMERGENCY SERVICES

Unless the practitioner is employed by a facility with comprehensive services and inpatient emergency care, it is necessary to proactively arrange for a source to which a client in crisis can be channeled. To minimize liability, the arrangement should include means for the clinician to have: (a) assurance that the client was, in fact, immediately accepted into care; (b) feedback about progress; and (c) notice when there is a major change of care (such as the client's being released from the emergency unit). Depending upon the clinician's degree of responsibility for the client, there may be a need to monitor the client's post-emergency situation.

Too many outpatient practitioners are prone to neglect making arrangements for emergency services. Indeed, depending upon the clientele, outpatient practitioners may have a duty to be available in emergencies, which could mean having a pager or an associate within the group practice being "on call" at all times.

Given the burden that around-the-clock availability creates, yet heeding the harbinger of liability from a duty to care for the client in an emergency, a precaution might be to issue a printed policy on emergencies to the client (and to important family members). This information should be provided to every client upon entry into the practice, thereby giving notice and gaining client acceptance for the practitioner's not being available for emergencies. The notice should include alternatives for emergency care, such as the names, addresses, and telephone numbers, along with admission criteria, of emergency units within the community. This policy and notice may or may not be adequate to reasonably meet the practitioner's duty to the client, but at least it is a step in the right direction.

GUIDELINE 41: HAVE A POLICY
FOR TERMINATION AND FOLLOW-UP

A malpractice cause of action can arise from a clinician's abandonment of a troubled client. Therefore, the mental health practitioner should have a plan for terminating clients and for making follow-up contacts.

To assure optimum legal usefulness, it is wise to have a policy about termination and follow-up that is, much like the previously discussed policy on emergency services, in writing and presented to every client (and to important family members) at the onset of treatment. Provision of a termination and follow-up policy creates a definite framework to counter any inferences of wrongful termination later on. If the policy states conditions for termination (such as noncompliance with treatment recommendations or failure to pay for services after a reasonable time) and the client entered treatment with knowledge of the conditions, the eventual termination would have a semblance of reasonableness, as is needed to meet the standard of care.

For the noncompliant client, policies should support that there is a mutual commitment: *The professional shall exercise his or her learned judgment about what will be the preferred treatment for the best interests of the client; and the client shall make a good-faith effort to fulfill the treatment recommendations and to make payment for service in a timely fashion.* If there is any doubt about the terms of this *quid pro quo* arrangement in the mind of either the client or the practitioner, it is unwise to provide services to the client. Allowing treatment to initiate or continue with a noncompliant client is tantamount to purposefully elevating the risk of malpractice. Obviously the refusal or discontinuation of treatment must be achieved tactfully and with an appropriate termination and/or referral plan.

A follow-up on the mental health welfare of the client documents that the practitioner demonstrated proper care for the client. As with virtually all dimensions of health care, it is advisable for follow-up efforts to be systematic. For example, it could be routine for the practitioner to contact every client a few weeks after the last scheduled appointment. This support will benefit the client's motivation for healthy living and the clinician's reputation—and the client will sense an open door to return to the practitioner whenever more help is needed.

If the mythical "prudent professional," from whom the standard of care is gleaned, would have sensed a reason to check up on a particular client subsequent to regular treatment, failure to do so could foster a complaint. For example, if the practitioner knew or should have known that the client was potentially dangerous and the client later committed suicide, a "wrongful death" malpractice action could be countered by a record of dutiful follow-up contacts with the client and earnest efforts to attain safeguards for the client (such as contacting family members and urging them to take precautions with the client).

GUIDELINE 42: IDENTIFY REFERRAL SOURCES

In support of effective termination and follow-up, it is worthwhile to have knowledge of where a particular type of client can obtain other professional services. Much like having an arrangement for emergency services for clients, the roster of available referral sources should be compiled before the press is on to find someplace to which, or someone to whom, the client can be directed. Last-minute efforts may be interpreted as faulty case management. It might seem that the practitioner is making an overdue effort for arrangements that should have been made at an earlier stage of treatment.

Any malpractice notion connected to abandonment can be countered by a client record that contains the clinician's: (a) efforts to gain a helpful termination; (b) recommendations for gaining services from other sources; and (c) contacts to verify that the client took steps to acquire the supplementary services. Likewise, a document of referral sources, with guidance for gaining admission, distributed to every client (which would be duly noted in the client record), exemplifies that the practitioner is conscientious and systematic in trying to further health and safety for all clients.

GUIDELINE 43: DO NOT ALLOW CLIENTS TO ACCRUE A DEFICIT IN PAYMENTS

Experience and reports from others support that the possibility of a malpractice compliant originates with a deficit in payment for service. It has long been believed that making payment yields a benefit to the client. By making a payment (perhaps regardless of amount), the client is motivated to cooperate with and benefit from the mental health treatment. It might even be speculated whether payment by a third-party, the health-insurance carrier, has deprived the client of a helpful condition of therapy. But it may go further. Lessening the client's responsibility for payment may, in turn, lead to resentment of having to make *any* payment.

Some practitioners foolishly rely on collecting the percentage of the cost of treatment paid by the health-insurance carrier with no intention of trying to collect the insured-client's portion. Some practitioners wrongfully tell their clients, "I will charge you $100, your health

121

insurance will pay $80 of it, and we'll just forget the other $20 that you are supposed to pay."

Such a practice is wrong and ill-advised. It is wrong because it amounts to fraud and has a deleterious effect on the client by demonstrating that even a mental health professional can exercise psychopathic thinking. It is ill-advised because this reveals the professional's character weakness to the client, and encourages him or her to attack for any unhealthy reason.

Many practitioners argue: "Some clients who can't afford to pay really need my help, and I don't mind forgetting their portion." Those clients may, indeed, need help, but public policy for health care does not support fraud for clients who cannot afford to pay for services. It supports their seeking services from publicly supported facilities or from practitioners with fees fixed at a level that they can afford.

There is ample evidence that as a deficit in payment rises, so too the likelihood of a malpractice claim rises. Given the clear-cut connection between a deficit in payment for service and a malpractice claim, it is foolhardy ("none of my clients would ever sue me") or just plain greedy ("I'll take what I can get from the health insurance—the carrier will never know that I dismiss the client's portion") to attempt to provide service to anyone who cannot afford it.

If the client cannot afford treatment, the practitioner may choose to serve the client, but not within a wrongful framework. Rather than risking malpractice by allowing a deficit in payment to accrue or being dishonest with the insurance carrier, the practitioner should either treat the client on a *pro bono* (gratis) basis, or refer the client to another treatment source that will provide services according to the client's ability to pay.

Chapter 8:
Healthy Defensiveness

Among mental health professionals, it is recognized that a client's ego-defense mechanisms are potentially both positive and negative. On the positive side, ego-defense mechanisms are essential for coping with emotional pressures. On the negative side, they sap much-needed strength and can reinforce unhealthy behavior.

There are times when it is healthy for a professional to be defensive—at least in business-related conduct. Litigious mental health clients necessitate that the practitioner exercise precautions, take proactive steps to avoid complaints, and behave personally and operate professionally in a manner that will counter conditions that could be a cause of action for malpractice.

GUIDELINE 44: FUNCTION AS A REASONABLE, ORDINARY, PRUDENT PRACTITIONER

By this point, it is obvious that avoiding malpractice is served by the practitioner's not being "wild and woolly" in either personal or professional conduct. Instead, the practitioner needs to plan well, be academically based, and be honorable in every clinical intervention. The standard of care must be maintained at all times.

Reasonable is defined by a mythical group of professional counterparts. While there is some leeway for defining a reference group, the composition must always support values that are viewed as "tried and true" by the eyes of society. Notwithstanding the idea that therapy is both an art and a science, the reasonable practitioner must be scholarly and, preferably, scientifically based in his or her services. Therefore, each client is treated according to an objectively determined and individualized plan.

Ordinary does not mean that there cannot be unique strategies. As discussed in the guideline on innovation and experimentation, the practitioner is free, even encouraged, to advance professional knowledge, but it must be pursued with controlled risk for the client. This means that new and unproven ideas must be subjected to progressive tests and pass peer review by other professionals. The advancement must also be in the best interest of the client, with informed consent, and conscionable to society.

Prudent can be defined several ways, not the least of which would be "cautious." It can be emotionally draining to be a mental health practitioner, and poor judgment can ensue. Any deviation from a formal professional-client relationship, regardless of reason, is especially risky for malpractice. Likewise, failure to "run a tight ship" with regard to office, personnel, and accounts management can lead to a collision with malpractice.

The standard of care for mental health practice, regardless of professional discipline or needs of the client, is inextricably tied to the practitioner's being reasonable, ordinary, and prudent. Perhaps an earlier day would have allowed the disciplines to wander around in search of definitions or alternatives for services, but a stage has been reached where all actors, both professionals and clients, are scripted to roles that are reviewed by public policy.

Unabashedly, the standard of care calls for professional defensiveness. Public policy wants reasonable, ordinary, and prudent conduct by practitioners, even at the risk of dampening enthusiasm for advances in treatment methods. Through allowing malpractice, public policy adds endorsement for the professional's being cautious. This public-policy stance leads to "protective practice," such as requiring special diagnostic services for all clients to undergird the legitimacy and suitability of the individually tailored treatment plan.

GUIDELINE 45: WHEN A COMPLAINT ARISES, REVERT TO A DEFENSIVE POSTURE

Mental health professionals espouse confronting conflicts. In therapy, there is logic for this belief. When practicing in a litigious era, it is foolish to try to confront a client with a complaint that can lead to a legal action.

Being legally safe supports that the professional must require each client to be compliant, at least in the sense of following treatment recommendations, policies for the practice, and so on. While the professional should encounter treatment noncompliance for the client's therapeutic growth, the treatment room is not the place to encounter a challenge that can find its way into a courtroom.

Any resistance by a client should be immediately scrutinized for its potential for strengthening a subsequent legal complaint. When a client refuses to be compliant, the professional should interpret it as a breach of the therapist-client alliance (i.e., a breach of the service contract). Self-integrity requires that the professional attempt to remedy the situation only as far as the therapeutic objectives allow. The therapeutic objectives cannot include dispute resolution of a legal nature.

As mentioned previously, the professional must be impeccably precise and honest. With acknowledged mental problems, the client can be expected to manipulate and play games. The practitioner can ill afford any blemish from wrongful thought or conduct. If the litigious client has discerned possible misconduct on the part of the practitioner, the only viable recourse is immediate reliance on legal counsel and a cessation of the professional contact with the client (with, of course, proper termination and referral).

Finally, the practitioner should not hesitate to pursue a legal remedy for his or her having been subjected to a complaint that is totally without merit and that represents a frivolous action intended to satisfy a pathological motive or to seek the "deep pocket" of the practitioner (or his or her malpractice-insurance carrier). Before making a judgment of this nature, it is necessary to weigh a number of considerations, and the assessment should have the help of thoughtful and competent legal counsel. (See Chapter 1 for comments on abuse of process and malicious prosecution.) The practitioner should harbor no reservations about pursuing a legal remedy simply because a former client is involved. Reservations should center on nonclient considerations, such as the financial cost of pursuing the matter and the possibility of generating adverse public attention to an already-ludicrous situation.

GUIDELINE 46: AVOID INDIGNATION
OR COYNESS WITH THE LEGAL SYSTEM

There are so many antitheses between the legal system and mental health services that it befuddles the minds of some mental health professionals to think that they cannot maneuver a solution to a client-related complaint (Slovenko, 1973). It should be remembered that a client with a complaint has, or soon will have, an ally: an attorney ready to advocate the client's interests. When a client obtains legal counsel, every word and act by the professional will potentially be grist for the malpractice mill.

Being aligned with intellectualizations, analyses, persuasion, and other mental gymnastics, the practitioner may respond to a query from a client's attorney with: "How dare you question my motives," or "If you want to play games, I'll match you wit for wit." Mental health professionals are trained for mental exercises, but attorneys are trained for mental combat.

In Chapter 4, a guideline encouraged the professional to learn to rely on allies, namely an attorney and accountant. When contacted by a client's attorney—no matter how innocuous it may seem on the surface—malpractice may be avoided by requesting that the attorney contact the practitioner's attorney. Under legal ethics and rules, an attorney must honor a request to deal with a designated attorney and thereafter abstain from contact with the party (the practitioner) without the presence of legal counsel.

Mental health professionals routinely charge for their services, but some are resistant to paying fees to other professionals for counsel, be it for business, accounting, or malpractice advice or representation. Given the career carnage from a malpractice skirmish, it is money well spent, no matter how limited the cross-fire, to obtain the services of a health care attorney (preferably one knowledgeable about mental health malpractice) when a client's attorney starts reconnoitering the client-care scene.

GUIDELINE 47: ELIMINATE SELF-
MANAGEMENT OF YOUR LEGAL CASE

Mental health professionals are trained to be in control of their treatment room. They are not, however, trained to be in control of the courtroom. Analysis of cases involving mental health professionals, keen of mind and with advanced academic training, supports that they are frequently their own worst enemies (Wright, 1981). Self-defeating behavior from the professional comes on in (at least) two ways: overtalk and overcontrol.

First, when face to face with an opposing attorney, the practitioner will often want to lock horns in verbal combat or try to explain away a minor wrongdoing. As mentioned earlier, mental health professionals might be able to lock horns with each other and have a fair fight on their own turf, but in the courtroom, they are locking horns with someone (the attorney) who is on his or her home field (some might liken it to matching a docile lap dog to a pit bulldog).

When being cross-examined, mental health professionals tend to try to construct a complex academic rationale for a fairly minor error. There is extensive research to document that judges and juries tune out and do not act favorably toward complex explanations. One attorney recently described his professional-client's "verbal suicide," saying: "I rehearsed with him over and over what he was supposed to say, explained why he should stick to simple facts, and he said he would do it—he got on the stand and from almost the first question on he jabbered away and dug a grave for himself."

Second, the intellectual, control-oriented professional may find it difficult, perhaps even impossible, to relinquish control to someone else, such as an attorney. Rather, the professional wants preemptive or veto rights for legal strategies. Coupled with the anxiety or pressure that is concomitant to litigation, this need to be in control often leads to dismissal of the attorney. "Changing horses in midstream" can be hazardous.

It is crucial to have an attorney upon whom trust and control can be placed. Granted, this necessitates thoughtful and thorough evaluation of qualities and competencies at the selection stage, but once an attorney has been retained, exacerbation of the negative consequences of a malpractice claim will best be avoided by allowing the legal expert to "drive the team."

GUIDELINE 48: AVOID OVEREXPOSURE OF PERSONAL QUALITIES AND OPINIONS

In some ways, the mental health professional lives in a fishbowl, with every movement or comment under the eye of critics. Being trained in human behavior, the mental health practitioner is supposed to "practice what he or she preaches" and set an example of healthy living.

The humanistic quest for authenticity by the therapist has merit, but it also has a risk attached. If the professional lives in a controversial or disreputable manner, what might have been a fairly minor error in clinical practice can be magnified or blown out of proportion—including in the courtroom. Although an egocentric voyage may be legitimate from the vantage point of human or constitutional rights, apostolic pursuit of certain areas of life can become an albatross for the practitioner. For example, certainly everyone is entitled to personal preferences in the realm of politics, religion, social issues, sexuality, and so on, but a practitioner with notoriety from involvement with one of these areas can prime a community to explode with the first spark of a malpractice complaint.

None of the foregoing means that the practitioner should be restrained from his or her rights and freedoms. To the contrary, health and fulfillment call for rigorous pursuit of personal interests, priorities, and need fulfillment. However, personal reputation can enter into a practitioner's legal vulnerability, whether at the formative stage for a cause of action or at the evidentiary stage before a jury.

To avoid malpractice, it may be necessary to "play it close to the vest." While it is unhealthy to live a lie, the vestment of professionalism makes it necessary for the practitioner to be discreet and to consider the ramifications of unconventional ideas and behavior.

Freedom of speech is one of our most sacred rights. The mental health professional should guard against the exercise of free speech turning into a stream of consciousness. Of special importance, care should constantly be maintained not to reveal confidences or speak about clients or other professionals. The World War II warning about spies listening for "loose tongues that will sink battleships" might be rephrased in this malpractice war to be "loose tongues will produce complaints."

GUIDELINE 49: SERVE STRICTLY AS A PROFESSIONAL TO YOUR CLIENTS

Mental health professionals are trained to handle therapeutically the transference-countertransference "phenomena." The high degree of emotion inherent in therapy can readily trigger personalized perceptions, which carry the potential for changing professional caring and sharing into nonprofessional feelings and behavior. When the latter occurs, public policy places liability onto the professional.

Public policy is reluctant to release the professional from the duty to safeguard the client. Therefore, it is no defense to assert that the client enticed the practitioner into an unprofessional relationship. For example, any sexual contact between a client and a mental health professional is prohibited, often by both criminal and civil law (Pope & Bouhoutsos, 1986). The latter may be manifested in an administrative action (e.g., by a state licensing board) or a tort (personal injury) action. To illustrate the impermeable professional framework imposed by public policy, the Florida Board of Psychological Examiners established a sexual misconduct rule that states, in part:

> The Board finds the effects of the psychologist-client relationship are powerful and subtle and that clients are influenced consciously and subconsciously by the unequal distribution of power inherent in such relationships. Furthermore, the Board finds that the effects of the psychologist-client relationship endure after psychological services cease to be rendered. Therefore, the client shall be presumed incapable of giving valid, informed, free consent to sexual activity involving the psychologist and the assertion of consent by the client shall not constitute a defense against charges of sexual misconduct. (Chapter 21U-15, p. 10)

The Board also sets forth a series of definitions and clarifications, and concludes: "For purposes of determining the existence of sexual misconduct as defined herein, the psychologist-client relationship is deemed to continue in perpetuity."

While sexual misconduct may provoke exceptional negativism, public policy is likely to apply the same principles to any form of alleged abuse of the professional-client relationship, regardless of the mental health discipline or the treatment circumstance. Ethical principles for every mental health discipline prescribe primary concern for preserving the welfare of the client, and proscribe any action by the professional (such as a relationship that creates a conflict of interest) that might jeopardize the client's welfare.

In practical terms, the foregoing means that there are clear-cut ethics and a less-clear, but still cogent, legal rationale for the professional's never forsaking the helping role with the client. As a rather mundane example, it is ill-advised, regardless of conditions, for a therapist ever to socialize with clients or former clients (if it can be practically avoided). Certain theories, especially of a humanistic bent, may view this matter differently, but the goal of avoiding malpractice is definitely furthered by an unrelenting retention of the formal professional relationship.

In the event of a malpractice complaint, public policy will probably be used as a basis for holding that the client is "incapable of giving valid, informed, free consent" to virtually any sort of act by the professional that allegedly led to injury to the client. Also, it seems likely that there is no period of time that can pass and eliminate the duties concomitant with the professional-client relationship.

Avoiding malpractice necessitates consistent and qualitative control of the professional-client relationship. Any inclination of moving across a professional boundary to a personal field would mean diminution of the primordial *raison d' être*, namely the best interests of the client through professional helping. Such a transition will surely meet with public-policy condemnation in the event of a complaint. Whether the connection be business, social, sexual, or whatever, there should be a permanent injunction against personalization and conflict of interest in the mind of the professional.

GUIDELINE 50: GUARD AGAINST THE SEVEN DEADLY SINS

Mental health professionals are quick to espouse holistic development of mind, body, and spirit for clients, but they are sometimes slow to make a self-application of the same principles. While there is no religious or theological intent, public policy does require a socio-philosophical morality of all health care providers. For centuries, sages have sermonized on how spiritual progress will be destroyed by the seven sins: pride, covetousness, lust, anger, gluttony, envy, and sloth. These sins are potentially no less fatal to career progress.

Every one of the classical sins can be associated with conduct that would receive societal disapproval. Given that this is the last guideline, an appropriate "Final Examination" might be for the reader to consider how each of the seven factors can create a problem in clinical practice, such as in the relationship between the therapist and client. It will take no late-night cramming to get a grade of 100%. There are a myriad of possibilities of professional-client problems that can occur if the relationship is infected by these negative conditions.

For mental health practitioners, these deadly sins may be reduced to the concept of greed. Analysis of malpractice cases reveals a common tendency for the errant practitioner to, at some point and in some way, conclude that he or she can escape sanction, or deserves special dispensation from standards required of other practitioners, or is above the law. This tendency often becomes manifest as conduct, by omission or commission, that points toward a definite motive of greed.

No matter how successful in practice, how advanced in training, or how many years of experience he or she has, every mental health professional must realize that he or she is a member of a discipline that is under the ever-vigilant scrutiny of society's monitors, be it an ethics committee, a state regulatory agency, or the legal system. Without exception, the intractable societal demand is for strict adherence to an acceptable standard of care.

References

American Psychological Association. (1981a). Ethical principles of psychologists. *American Psychologist, 36,* 633-638.

American Psychological Association. (1981b). Specialty guidelines for the delivery of services. *American Psychologist, 36,* 639-681.

American Psychological Association. (1987). General guidelines for providers of psychological services. *American Psychologist, 42,* 712-723.

Anderson, J. E. (1979). *Public Policy-Making: Decisions and Their Implementation* (2nd ed.). New York: Holt, Rinehart and Winston.

AuClaire, P. A. (1984). Public attitudes toward social welfare expenditures. *Social Work, 29,* 139-144.

Baker, J. W., II. (1983). Continuing professional development. In C. E. Walker (Ed.), *The Handbook of Clinical Psychology* (Volume II, pp. 1351-1374). Homewood, IL: Dow Jones-Irwin.

Bartol, C. R. (1983). *Psychology and American Law.* Belmont, CA: Wadsworth.

Belli, M. (1980). Loss of consortium: Academic addendum or substantial right? *Trial, 16,* 73-75.

Besharov, D. J. (1985). *The Vulnerable Social Worker: Liability for Serving Children and Families.* Silver Spring, MD: National Association of Social Workers.

Bice, T. W. (1981). Social science and health services: Contributions to public policy. In J. B. McKinlay (Ed.),

Issues in Health Care Policy (pp. 1-28). Cambridge, MA: The MIT Press.

Bierig, J. R. (1983). Whatever happened to professional self-regulation? *American Bar Association Journal, 69,* 616-619.

Blackburn, J. D., Klayman, E. I., & Malin, M. H. (1982). *Legal Environment of Business: Public Law and Regulation.* Homewood, IL: Richard D. Irwin.

Blankenship, G. (1986, June 15). Study shows million dollar awards hard to collect. *The Florida Bar News, 13*(12), 5.

Blodgett, N. (1985). Forced insurance. *American Bar Association Journal, 71,* 37.

Bowen, H. R., & Jeffers, J. R. (1971). *The Economics of Health Services.* New York: General Learning Press.

Caplan, G. (1970). *The Theory and Practice of Mental Health Consultation.* New York: Basic Books.

Etzioni, A. (Ed.). (1969). *The Semi-Professions and Their Organization.* New York: Free Press.

Fein, R. (1981). Social and economic attitudes shaping American health policy. In J. B. McKinlay (Ed.), *Issues in Health Care Policy* (pp. 29-65). Cambridge, MA: The MIT Press.

Fieger, G. N. (1987). Medical malpractice tort reform: An analysis and comparison of existing acts. *Michigan Bar Journal, 66,* 262-267.

Fischer, L., & Sorenson, G. P. (1985). *School Law for Counselors, Psychologists, and Social Workers.* New York: Longman.

Fisher, K. (1985). Charges catch clinicians in cycle of shame, slip-ups. *American Psychological Association Monitor, 16,* 6-7.

Florida Bar. (1987, April 1). 80% of public view courts as overworked. *The Florida Bar News, 14*(7), 11.

Francis, B. (1987, February 1). Malpractice issue pains area's doctors, patients. *Fort Myers News-Press,* Section A, pp. 1, 6-7.

Glenn, R. D. (1974). Standard of care in administering non-traditional psychotherapy. *University of California, Davis Law Review, 7,* 56-83.

Hallerstein, D. (1984, July). *Harpers,* p. 74.

Harshbarger, D., & Demone, H. W., Jr. (1982). Impact of public policy on mental health services. In H. C. Schulberg & M. Killilea (Eds.), *The Modern Practice of Community Mental Health* (pp. 230-245). San Francisco: Jossey-Bass.

Hobbs, N. (1964). Mental health's third revolution. *American Journal of Orthopsychiatry, 34,* 822-833.

Hogan, D. B. (1979). *The Regulation of Psychotherapists. Volume III. A Review of Malpractice Suits in the United States.* Cambridge, MA: Ballinger.

Holmes, O. W., Jr. (1966). An analysis of the standard of care. In L. Wolfstone (Ed.), *Personal Injury Liability* (Volume I, pp. 3-7). Ann Arbor, MI: Institute of Continuing Legal Education. (The chapter is comprised of extracts from an article that appeared in *The Common Law,* Lecture III: Torts-trespass and negligence, 1881)

Jacobs, H. B. (1978). *The Spectre of Malpractice.* Herndon, VA: The Medical Quality Foundation.

Jacobs, H. B. (1986). *Understanding Medical Malpractice.* Herndon, VA: The Medical Quality Foundation.

James, F., Jr. (1966). The qualities of the reasonable man in negligence cases. In L. L. Wolfstone (Ed.), *Personal Injury Liability* (Volume I, pp. 9-35). Ann Arbor, MI: Institute of Continuing Legal Education. (This chapter originally appeared in the *Missouri Law Review, 16,* 1-26, 1951).

Joint Commission on Mental Illness and Health. (1961). *Action for Mental Health.* New York: Basic Books.

Keeton, W. P., Dobbs, D. B., Keeton, R. E., & Owen, D. G. (1984). *Prosser and Keeton on the Law of Torts* (5th ed.). St. Paul, MN: West.

Kerlinger, F. N. (1964). *Foundation of Behavioral Research.* New York: Holt, Rinehart and Winston.

King, J. H., Jr. (1977). *The Law of Medical Malpractice.* St. Paul, MN: West.

Kionka, E. J. (1977). *Torts: Injuries to Person and Property.* St. Paul, MN: West.

Knapp, S., & VandeCreek, L. (1981). Behavioral medicine: Its malpractice risks for psychologists. *Professional Psychology, 12,* 677-683.

Lee County Bar Association/Lee County Medical Society. (1986). *Lee County Medical-Legal Code.* Fort Myers, FL: Authors.

Leesfield, I. H. (1987). Negligence of mental health professionals. *Trial, 23,* 57-61.

Magaro, P. A., Gripp, R., & McDowell, D. J. (1978). *The Mental Health Industry.* New York: John Wiley & Sons.

Marvell, T. B., & Dempsey, P. M. (1985). Growth in state judgeships, 1970-1984: What factors are important? *Judicature, 68,* 274-284.

References

McCarthy, C. (1986). Lawyer's effort to help not understood. *American Trial Lawyers Association Advocate, 12,* 2.

Mechanic, D. (1981). Some dilemmas in health care policy. In J. B. McKinlay (Ed.), *Issues in Health Care Policy* (pp. 80-94). Cambridge, MA: The MIT Press.

Monahan, J. (1983). The prediction of violent behavior: Developments in psychology and law. In C. J. Scheirer & B. L. Hammonds (Eds.), *Psychology and the Law* (pp. 147-176). Washington, DC: American Psychological Association.

Olle, D. J., & Macaulay, R. B. (1986). General partnerships. In Florida Bar Continuing Legal Education Committee (Ed.), *Florida Small Business Practice* (pp. 61-82). Tallahassee, FL: The Florida Bar.

Overcast, T. D., & Sales, B. D. (1981). Psychological and multidisciplinary corporations. *Professional Psychology, 12,* 749-760.

Palagi, R. J., & Springer, J. R. (1984). Personal injury law. In R. H. Woody (Ed.), *The Law and the Practice of Human Services* (pp. 155-198). San Francisco: Jossey-Bass.

Perlman, P. (1986). Unmasking the fox. *Trial, 22,* 5-6.

Pope, K. S., & Bouhoutsos, J. C. (1986). *Sexual Intimacy between Therapists & Patients.* New York: Praeger.

Proffer, L. (1987). Coping with a crisis. *Michigan Bar Journal, 66,* 268-272.

Prosser, W. L. (1971). *Handbook of the Law of Torts* (4th ed.). St. Paul, MN: West.

Reardon, L. (1985, December 26). Malpractice insurance woes: Nebraska professionals face high rates, fewer policies. *Omaha World-Herald,* p. 43.

Richards, G. (1984, September). Malpractice losses are building--again. *Hospitals,* pp. 108 & 110.

Roach, W. J., Jr., Chernoff, S. N., & Esley, C. L. (1985). *Medical Records and the Law.* Rockville, MD: Aspen Systems.

Rossi, P. H., Wright, J. D., Fisher, G. A., & Willis, G. (1987). The urban homeless: Estimating composition and size. *Science, 235,* 1336-1341.

Rychlak, J. F. (1968). *A Philosophy of Science for Personality Theory.* Boston: Houghton-Mifflin.

Saywell, R. M., Jr., & McHugh, G. J. (1986). Organization of the health care delivery system in the U.S. In G. T. Troyer & S. L. Salman (Eds.), *Handbook of Health Care*

References

Risk Management (pp. 1-52). Rockville, MD: Aspen Systems.

Schutz, B. M. (1982). *Legal Liability in Psychotherapy.* San Francisco: Jossey-Bass.

Shelton, D. E., Bishop, L. R., & Blaske, T. H. (1987). 1986 tort reform legislation: A summary. *Michigan Bar Journal, 66,* 252-260.

Slovenko, R. (1973). *Psychiatry and Law.* Boston: Little, Brown.

Starkman, S. (1978). Sociological criteria of professionalization with comments regarding school psychology. In J. L. Carroll (Ed.), *Contemporary School Psychology* (pp. 58-65). Brandon, VT: Clinical Psychology Publishing.

Stavro, B. (1986, March 10). Risk is relative. *Forbes,* p. 63.

Trent, C. L. (1978). Psychiatric malpractice insurance and its problems: An overview. In W. E. Barton & C. J. Sanborn (Eds.), *Law and the Mental Health Professions* (pp. 101-117). New York: International Universities Press.

Turkington, C. (1984). Women therapists not immune to sexual involvement suits. *American Psychological Association Monitor, 14*(12), 15.

Turkington, C. (1986a). Response to crisis: Pay up or go naked. *American Psychological Association Monitor, 17*(4), 6-7.

Turkington, C. (1986b). Suit data show no need to panic. *American Psychological Association Monitor, 17*(11), 9.

Verrillo, M. (1987). Alabama Blue Cross charges counselors with fraud. *American Association for Counseling and Development Guidepost, 29,* 1, 8, 11.

Walters, H. A. (1980). Dangerousness. In R. H. Woody (Ed.), *The Encyclopedia of Clinical Assessment* (Vol. II, pp. 1104-1111). San Francisco: Jossey-Bass.

Wigmore, J. (1935). *A Students' Textbook of the Law of Evidence.* Chicago: Foundation Press.

Wilkinson, A. P. (1982). Psychiatric malpractice: Identifying areas of liability. *Trial, 18,* 73-77, 89-90.

Woody, J. D., & Woody, R. H. (1988). Public policy in life-threatening situations. *Journal of Marital and Family Therapy, 14,* 133-137.

Woody, R. H. (1971). *Psychobehavioral Counseling and Therapy: Integrating Behavioral and Insight Techniques.* New York: Appleton-Century-Crofts.

Woody, R. H. (Ed.). (1984). *The Law and the Practice of Human Services.* San Francisco: Jossey-Bass.

References

Woody, R. H. (1985a). Public policy, malpractice law, and the mental health professional: Some legal and clinical guidelines. In C. P. Ewing (Ed.), *Psychology, Psychiatry, and the Law: A Clinical and Forensic Handbook* (pp. 509-525). Sarasota, FL: Professional Resource Exchange, Inc.

Woody, R. H. (1985b). Shaping public policy for family health. In J. R. Springer & R. H. Woody (Eds.), *Health Promotion in Family Therapy* (pp. 1-12). Rockville, MD: Aspen Systems.

Woody, R. H. (1988). *Protecting Your Mental Health Practice.* San Francisco: Jossey-Bass.

Woody, R. H., & Mitchell, R. E. (1984). Understanding the legal system and legal research. In R. H. Woody (Ed.), *The Law and the Practice of Human Services* (pp. 1-38). San Francisco: Jossey-Bass.

Wright, R. H. (1981). What to do until the malpractice lawyer comes: A survivor's manual. *American Psychologist, 36,* 1535-1541.

Index

If You'd Like to Know More . . .

Dear Customer:

Fifty Ways to Avoid Malpractice: A Guidebook for Mental Health Professionals is only one of many publications and continuing education programs offered by the Professional Resource Exchange, Inc.

If you would like to receive more information on our publications, please call us (**Toll Free 1-800-443-3364**) or write (Professional Resource Exchange, Inc., P.O. Box 15560, Sarasota, FL 34277-1560), and we will be happy to send you our latest catalog. When you call or write, please tell us your professional training (e.g., Psychologist, Clinical Social Worker, Marriage and Family Therapist, Mental Health Counselor, School Psychologist, Psychiatrist, etc.) to be assured of receiving all appropriate mailings.

We are dedicated to providing you, the mental health professional, with applied resources and up-to-date information that you can immediately use in your practice. Our orders are usually shipped within 2 working days and come with a 15 day no-questions-asked money back guarantee.

Thanks for your interest!

Sincerely,

Lawrence G. Ritt, PhD
President